BENEATH THE WAVES

Library and Archives Canada Cataloguing in Publication

Vautier, Clarence, 1972-
    Beneath the waves : Newfoundland sea stories / Clarence Vautier.

Includes index.
ISBN 978-1-894463-97-3

    1. Seafaring life--Newfoundland and Labrador--History.
2. Shipwrecks--Newfoundland and Labrador--History. I. Title.

FC2161.8.V38 2006   971.8   C2006-902369-7

MIX
Paper from
responsible sources
FSC
www.fsc.org   **FSC® C016245**

This paper has been certified to meet the envi-
ronmental and social standards of the Forest
Stewardship Council® (FSC®) and comes
from responsibly managed forests, and veri-
fied recycled sources.

PRINTED IN CANADA

FLANKER PRESS
PO BOX 2522, STATION C
ST. JOHN'S, NL, CANADA
TOLL FREE: 1-866-739-4420
WWW.FLANKERPRESS.COM

Cover Design by Margot Gordon
First Canadian edition printed May 2006

9 8 7 6

Canada   Canada Council   Conseil des Arts   Newfoundland
                for the Arts   du Canada   Labrador

We acknowledge the financial support of the Government of Canada through the Canada Book Fund (CBF) and the
Government of Newfoundland and Labrador, Department of Business, Tourism, Culture and Rural Development for our
publishing activities. We acknowledge the support of the Canada Council for the Arts, which last year invested $153
million to bring the arts to Canadians throughout the country. *Nous remercions le Conseil des arts du Canada de son
soutien. L'an dernier, le Conseil a investi 153 millions de dollars pour mettre de l'art dans la vie des Canadiennes et
des Canadiens de tout le pays.*

BENEATH THE WAVES

NEWFOUNDLAND SEA STORIES

Clarence Vautier

FLANKER PRESS LTD.
ST. JOHN'S, NL
2006

Dedication

To Brandon and Hannah, my two precious children.

TABLE OF CONTENTS

INTRODUCTION

In 2001, AFTER COUNTLESS PERSONAL INTERVIEWS AND PAINSTAKING research, I published a collection of short stories entitled *The Coast of Newfoundland: The Southwest Corner.* Since that time, I've had the fortune of meeting and conversing with more wonderful people who were eager to share their stories and memories. These recollected pieces of the past involved shipwrecks, family tragedies, collisions at sea, and much more. As with the first compilation, I felt that these people also deserved to have their stories told.

In many situations, the records of these occurrences were limited, however people were gracious in offering documentation, photos, and whatever information they felt could be useful.

My hope is that by reading this book, some other young writer's interest in local history will be stimulated, which in turn, will help preserve the history of the hardworking people of Newfoundland and Canada's east coast.

The knowledge I have gained in researching and writing these stories has been tremendous. I hope the reader will enjoy them as much as I enjoyed presenting it.

Clarence Vautier

The Mystery of the Maud Gilliam

Between the southwest point of Newfoundland at Cape Ray and the north point of Cape Breton called Cape North, there lies a stretch of open water some sixty miles wide. The area known as the Cabot Strait has been a busy shipping lane for commercial ships and fishing vessels for decades.

Although this stretch of water is only sixty miles wide, it has, over the years, claimed hundreds of lives in a variety of different ways. Many of the lives lost in this area have been from coasting schooners and fishing boats, that in some cases, have simply vanished without a trace.

In the fall of 1894, Captain Michael Gilliam of Channel, Newfoundland, prepared for another routine voyage to Cape Breton in his schooner the *Maud Gilliam*. The *Maud Gilliam* was a 76-foot schooner built in Shelburne, Nova Scotia, in 1889, and was owned by Captain Gilliam himself. Gilliam was an experienced hand in the coasting trade and had many voyages in the waters of the Cabot Strait and beyond.

On the morning of November 22, 1894, the *Maud Gilliam* slipped her lines and departed Channel for the 95-mile voyage to North Sydney to pick up a cargo of coal and general supplies for the local merchants around Channel. In a short while, the *Maud Gilliam* passed Channel Head and headed into the open water. There were also other schooners from the Channel area destined for the same port with similar cargo.

Later that night the weather began to change, with an increase in winds and sea, along with poor visibility. People back home knew that the schooners and their crews must have had an uncomfortable night, but no one really felt concerned for the fleet of schooners.

As time passed, the *Maud Gilliam* was the only schooner unheard from. Family members began to ask questions and wonder were the vessel was. Unfortunately there were no answers to their questions. The *Maud Gilliam* and her crew had simply vanished.

What could have happened to the crew and the sturdy vessel will always be a mystery, yet one still ponders the question.

The *Maud Gilliam* was similar to other vessels crossing the Cabot Strait from Port aux Basques that night. If the weather had overcome the vessel, why hadn't other vessels in the fleet experienced trouble as well? At the time of the incident, the vessel was still new, just five years old, and built by some of the best-known shipbuilders in Shelburne. By the time the weather had gotten bad she would have been close to the Cape Breton shores, yet there was no wreckage, survivors, or bodies found. Maybe the *Maud Gilliam* and her crew were involved in a collision with a large commercial ship shortly after leaving Channel, and the wreckage drifted past the remote coastline of the Channel area and into the vast waters of the Gulf of St. Lawrence.

The *Maud Gilliam* and her crew had joined the long list of those lost at sea. At the time of her disappearance her crew and passengers were as follows:

Michael Gilliam, 55	John Gilliam, 22
Philip Gilliam, 22	James Sheaves, 28
Keiz Carter, 50	Alexander Waddell, 32
Benjamin Gilliam, 57	Marie Gillingham, 27

The Wreck of the Fiona

O ver the past century, there have been incidents involving freak waves and storms that seem to come out of nowhere. With today's technology and continuous research, most of these events are forecast ahead of time, avoiding disasters at sea and on land.

Still, this was not the case in September of 1900, when the whole continent of North America was affected by an irregular weather pattern. The week had started out fine. In the eastern portion of the Caribbean, a normal, seasonal hurricane had developed, and was slowly making its way westward. Unfortunately, before long, Hurricane Isaac gathered great strength as it made its way north.

The hurricane season in the North American quadrant of the world runs from June to November. These hurricanes develop in the warm waters of the Caribbean and travel westward until they reach the northern latitude of approximately 20°. Here they turn with the effect of the prevailing westerlies and travel eastward towards the eastern seaboard of North America. Oftentimes, they pass far enough to the east so that Nova Scotia and Newfoundland avoid getting the brunt of it.

A hurricane has to have certain features to maintain its true character and one of these characteristics is that they must maintain a water temperature of twenty-five degrees celsius. Shortly after a hurricane makes contact with land, it either veers away or simply diminishes due to the fall in water temperature.

On September 8, 1900, Hurricane Isaac touched land near Texas, but continued northward towards Canada. It changed direction, but its intensity remained the same. This was unusual and on the morning of September 13, 1900, the hurricane swept over the East Coast of Canada and onward towards Newfoundland.

The results of the storm were devastating. On land it carried away houses and caused floods resulting in loss of life. Closer to home, the results were much the same. The fishermen on the fishing grounds had no idea that such a storm was approaching and thus were oblivious to the danger.

Captain Joseph Vatcher was in command of the 49-foot fishing skiff *Lizzie*. On the morning the storm swept over the south and southwest coast, the *Lizzie* was fishing somewhere in the vicinity of Burgeo Bank. The crew: Captain Vatcher, Hugh Dominey, Charles Hann, Harry Parsons, George V. Rose, Henry Dicks, Joseph Gunnery, and a Mr. Simms, were never seen again.

As weeks passed, people began to accept the loss of their loved ones. On the morning of October 15, 1900, fishermen in La Poile and West Point were carrying out their normal activities when they came upon the green hull of a overturned schooner. The vessel was floating with its bow submerged and stern portion floating just above the surface.

The fishermen became very curious about the identity of schooner, and even more so, about the whereabouts of the crew. Were they close by in a dory, or along the shoreline waiting to be rescued? They knew someone had come upon the derelict earlier because there were several small holes cut through the bottom planking.

The fishermen decided they would pull the wreck ashore in the hope of identifying it, and to see if there were any bodies inside. Unfortunately they ran into problems trying to get the schooner ashore because its anchor was entangled in the ocean floor and still attached to the vessel. With the bow submerged they had difficulty cutting the chain free.

After days and days of trying, they finally cleared the anchor and towed the schooner ashore. Once on land, the vessel was identified as the *Fiona,* which hailed from the French Islands of St. Pierre and

Miquleon. The *Fiona* had just been given up for lost when the vessel was caught in the same storm as the *Lizzie* that swept through the area just a month previous on September 13, 1900.

Once the schooner was finally ashore, the fishermen cut holes in the bottom to see if any bodies remained inside. In the hold of the schooner, they discovered that the bulkhead was missing, and the debris inside had shifted forward and caused the schooner to sink by the bow.

After searching the remainder of the schooner, they discovered three bodies. After further examination, they found that the bodies were those of two men, and the third, according to the size and remaining features, was that of a teenager. The bodies were then taken to West Point where they were dressed and placed in coffins. Finally on October 22, 1900, they were laid to rest after a short service by Eldred Gosse of Petites.

Tragedy at East Bay

In the mid-1800s, looking for another life in the new world, the number of immigrants from England and France coming to the south and southwest coast was rising. Some of these people went to the larger outports to live, and others went where no one had yet settled. Its result was that the coves and bays along the southwest and south coast consisted of little outports, some not much more than a mile apart. These communities, big or small, were totally isolated from each other, until the early 1900s, when the newly founded Reid Steamship Company introduced ferries that visited the larger ports along the coast to bring food, mail, passengers, and so on.

La Poile Bay in the early 1900s was one such case. It saw some of its first settlers in the early 1800s, and as time progressed, the bay consisted of upward of a dozen communities such as Bevan's Cove, Round Harbour, East Bay, Dolman's Cove, North Bay, Northwest Cove (Broad Cove), and La Plante.

Although La Poile consisted of many ports, the ferry only visited the largest of them, La Poile Harbour. As for the remainder of the residents in La Poile Bay, when it came time to pick up supplies, they would have to use their own means of transportation.

Two of the larger communities located within La Poile Bay (besides La Poile Harbour) were East Bay and North Bay, both named after their geographical direction. Eastern Bay was first settled, sometime in the early 1860s, by residents from another community to the west of La Poile named West Point. North Bay was similarly settled only thirty years later. Between East Bay and

—6—

North Bay there was one other settlement named Dolman's Cove. There, the residents consisted of one family, George and Hannah Taylor, along with their children.

Because the residents from all three communities were related, they would often travel back and forth by rowboat to visit their loved ones. Although the distance was short, and the bays were well protected, tragedy still occurred.

October 29, 1921, was a typical fall day in the isolated communities of La Poile Bay, and fifteen-year-old George Taylor (Jr.) decided to visit his sister Louise at East Bay. Louise was just twelve years old at the time and was living at East Bay with Thomas and Emma MacDonald, along with their three sons and one daughter Hattie, William, Philip, and John.

Shortly after noon on October 29, two of the MacDonald brothers, Philip and John, were preparing to take George back to his home in nearby Dolman's Cove, just two miles away. The means of transportation was a small rowboat fitted with a sail that was owned by the MacDonald family.

Not long after the three boys departed the wharf, a strong squall of northeast wind blew down from the high hilltops and through the valley of East Bay. A gust of wind suddenly struck the rowboat, and in an instant, the boat capsized, throwing the men into the water. The three men were left fighting for their lives.

George Jr. and John MacDonald had managed to hold onto the bottom of the overturned rowboat, but Philip MacDonald was not as fortunate. After a short while, and before help could arrive, John could hold on no longer. He finally slipped beneath the surface and drowned.

William MacDonald and his father Thomas had seen the accident from their house on shore just moments after it happened. As a result, they took a small boat and headed for the distressed young men. When William and his father arrived on the scene, George Taylor Jr. was alive and hanging onto the overturned boat, but his two sons were nowhere to be seen. He also knew that during this time of year, the survival time in such cold water would be short.

East Bay, where the three young men were trying to cross. (Author's Collection).

After George Taylor Jr. was taken ashore, William and his father were left to search for the MacDonald brothers. The small waves caused by the wind made it difficult to see beneath the surface. With the wind blowing off the hills and the current from the river at East Bay, the two brothers would be swept out of the bay into deeper water before long. After hours of searching, the two men returned home with no luck.

The next day, the news of the tragedy had reached North Bay. Many of the residents pledged their sorrow, but knew there was little they could do, except one man, local boat builder Josiah Farrell. He thought that there was a possibility that the bodies may still be in the vicinity of the accident.

With this in mind he had a suggestion. He took a wooden barrel (mostly likely a puncheon) and cut it in half with a small hole in one side. Over the hole he placed a piece of glass. By this method he could put the barrel overboard and see clearly beneath the surface without the effect of the waves.

The barrel was taken to East Bay to see if they could find the bodies of the two brothers. They started to search in the area where the boat had capsized, and after a short while, they found the body of John MacDonald (aged eighteen), the oldest of the two brothers. They then resumed the search for Philip MacDonald.

Philip MacDonald (left) and John MacDonald (right) on the wharf in Grand Bruit awaiting burial. (Photo courtesy of Florence Francis).

Not long after, the body of Philip MacDonald (aged fifteen) was recovered. The two bodies were carried ashore and dressed. From East Bay they were taken to Grand Bruit and buried in the local cemetery.

The Wreck of the Donald L. Silver

The island of Newfoundland has always been known for its fishery, that mainly being cod. However, on the west coast, the herring fishery has been a thriving industry since the late 1800s. The concentration of that fishery has primarily been in the Bay of Islands area.

The communities along the Bay of Islands have fished herring since they settled there. The fishery grew rapidly because the herring was used as bait to catch cod and shellfish, and also processed in several different ways for consumption.

Like other ports that experience prosperous industries, the herring fishery in the Bay of Islands drew fishermen in from other areas. It didn't take long for some fishermen to become merchants, who set up large businesses to purchase and process the herring, and then deliver it to other ports.

One of the largest and best-known firms to come to the Bay of Islands area was the Gorthon Pew Company of Gloucester, Massachusetts. They dealt in pickled and smoked herring, as well as, salted and dried cod.

One family, which was well-known and still is today in the herring fishery is the Hackett family from English Harbour East, Fortune Bay. They resettled in the Bay of Islands area in the early 1900s. Two members of the Hackett family were Captain John Hackett and his brother Captain Joseph Hackett. John A. Hackett relocated to Woods Island while Joseph Hackett relocated to Lower Summerside. Both communities are located on the north side of the Bay of Islands, and Woods Island is where the Gorthon Pew Company is also located.

The Hackett brothers were well-respected and skilled navigators who commanded large schooners. Their trade often saw themselves coasting along the east coast of Canada and the United States. Oftentimes, the brothers carried herring from Woods Island to Gloucester for the Gorthon Pew Company.

In the fall of 1923, Captain Joseph Hackett was in command of a 105-foot schooner name the *Donald L. Silver*, and was again chartered by the Gorthon Pew Company to carry a cargo of salted herring from the Bay of Islands to Gloucester.

With the herring season coming to a close in December of 1923, there were only a few vessels anchored in the Bay of Islands. Two of the ships anchored were local schooners, the *Donald L. Silver*, under the Captain Joseph Hackett, and the *Lucille Smith*, under command of Captain Michael Hackett.

On December 28, 1923, the *Donald L. Silver* finished loading

her cargo at Middle Arm and sailed to the nearby community of Woods Island. Upon arrival, the captain's brother, Captain John Hackett, joined the crew. Once the cargo of herring was delivered, Captain Joseph Hackett was planning on returning home to spend some time with his family and Captain John Hackett was to take command of the the vessel.

The *Donald L. Silver* was moored at the berth in Woods Island for several days, which gave the crew a chance to spend some time with their families before leaving on the winter voyage.

James Hackett.
(Photo courtesy of John L. Hackett).

Finally on December 31, 1923, the captain cleared customs for the foreign voyage the next day.

On New Year's Day, 1924, the two captains attended the church service, and before boarding the schooner, they stopped to say goodbye to the custom's officer I. M Costello. Because it was near lunchtime, the custom's officer and his wife offered the two gentlemen lunch and they agreed.

Shortly after eating, with a light wind and an ebb tide, the glorious looking schooner departed Woods Island. With such little wind, it would take the *Donald L. Silver* until nearly dark when she cleared the entrance of the bay into the open water of the Gulf of St. Lawrence.

The first night of the voyage went well with a light southeast wind and mild temperatures, but this changed abruptly in the early afternoon of the next day. By the early evening of January 2, the wind had increased to gale force, reaching over seventy knots, while the temperature dropped severely. Many of the local residents in the Port au Port area say it was one of the worst storms they had ever seen. The families and friends back on shore knew that the *Donald L. Silver* and her crew must have experienced a terrible night.

In the early evening, residents in the St. George's area thought they saw what appeared to be a two-masted schooner. No one would have imagined that this was the *Donald L. Silver* because by this time the vessel should have been well into the Cabot Strait and south of Newfoundland.

As dawn rose on the morning of January 3, residents in the area of Bank Head on the south side of St. George's Bay, and south of the Bay of Islands, discovered wreckage of a schooner on a nearby beach. It was soon discovered that the remains belonged to the *Donald L. Silver.*

The residents who discovered the flotsam noticed that some of the wreckage was above the high water mark. It appeared that the crew had tried to beach the schooner in the hope of saving their lives. The end result was that the schooner probably hit a reef just off the beach because the forward section of the schooner, including the windlass, was all in one piece.

There is support for the theory that the crew may have tried to beach the schooner because two of the crew of the *Donald L. Silver* knew this area well for the simple fact they were born and raised there. The residents also noticed that the mast of the schooner had axe marks on it. Hence they must have attempted to chop the spars free in the hope of saving the schooner

Unfortunately, whatever attempts they tried were futile, for shortly after discovering the wreckage, the bodies of four crew members were found. They were: Alonzo Wheeler aged twenty-three; William Ruth aged twenty-one of Summerside; Harold Swyers aged thirty-four; and his brother Frank aged forty-nine, both of Sandy Point, Bay St. George.

The body of Joseph Hackett aged forty-five was found a few days later. He was buried at Curling on January 12, 1924. Left to mourn were his wife Margaret and their five children. The body of John A. Hackett, aged forty-three was found in the ice on January 11, 1924, at Bank Head by Max Benoit, and buried on January 15, 1924, at Woods Island.

By mid-January, all of the bodies with the exception of mate, James Hackett were recovered. Elizabeth Hackett, mother of James, although bedridden, prayed continuously for her son's body to be found. Then one day in late February, after finishing her prayers, she got the news that her son was found. He was buried on March 2, 1924, at Woods Island. He was only twenty-six.

Captain Joseph Hackett on deck of the
SV *Donald L. Silver*
(Photo courtesy of John L. Hackett).

For the family of Joseph Hackett, the sorrow was far from over. Just two years after Joseph Hackett drowned, his oldest daughter Theresa, at fifteen years, died on December 4, 1925. Just two months later, on February 6, 1926, the widow of Joseph Hackett passed away as well. Other members of the Hackett family raised the remaining two girls and one son, Joseph Hackett, who was just a toddler at the time of his father's death.

Tragedy at Grand Bruit

The southwest coast of Newfoundland experienced its first transportation development in the late 1890s and early 1900s with the formation of the Reid Steamship Company. Since then, transportation has dramatically changed and improved. The days of large ferries making ports of call from Port aux Basques as far eastward as Fortune Bay have passed, and smaller ferries have taken their place. Although 100 years or more has passed, and things have improved, there are still times when people use their own means of transportation to visit the larger ports. This was often the case when people had to be at certain places at specific times.

In the summer of 1926, Hazel Billard was a young lady growing up in the community of Grand Bruit, some forty miles east of Port aux Basques. Hazel was a willing and energetic young lady who wanted to go elsewhere to look for work, but in order to get to the mainland, she would have to travel to Port aux Basques to get passage on one of the Reid Passenger ferries which would take her to North Sydney. However, getting to Port aux Basques from Grand Bruit in 1926 was very difficult.

Fortunately, Hazel was in luck when two fishermen from Grand Bruit named Thomas Billard and William Neil offered their fishing skiff, the *Florence*, to anyone who wished to carry Hazel westward to make connections with the Reid passenger ferries. On the morning of August 5, 1926, Hazel boarded the *Florence* crewed by Harvey James and Hebert Billard.

Thomas and William didn't want to lose a day of fishing, so they decided they would fish the day in a rowboat. The *Florence* departed

Grand Bruit and the two fishermen boarded their small boat. The fishing grounds were not far, just over a mile in an area known as Bad Neighbour. Fishing in an area close by was a fisherman from Grand Bruit named Howard Miles.

As Thomas Billard and William Neil were setting their trawl, a sudden gust of wind blowing off the high hilltops, suddenly hit their rowboat and swamped it. Before the men had realized what happened, they found themselves fighting for their lives. The fishermen were fortunate enough to have gotten hold of the rowboat, but they could not hold on for long.

As mentioned earlier, Howard Miles was not far from the fishermen. Witnessing their misfortune, the lone fisherman tried everything in his might to reach the stricken two. He managed to reach the location where the boat had capsized, but unfortunately the two fishermen were nowhere to be seen.

When the news reached back home in Grand Bruit, the residents searched the coves, islands, and beaches, but there was no sign of the fishermen. The bodies of the two men were mostly likely carried out to sea by the wind and current. Both Thomas Billard and William Neil were married with children.

Sometime later, the swamped rowboat was found. It was discovered several miles to the westward near the community of West Point.

The next year, the sons of Thomas Billard were left without the help and knowledge of their father. With their mother and siblings still relatively young, the brothers decided to order the building of a skiff from

Fishermen of Grand Bruit in the 1920s. (L-R) Cecil Billard, Walter Billard, and Thomas Billard. (Photo courtesy of the late Fred Ingram).

MV *Billard Brothers* and the MV *Thomas Marie* in Grand Bruit Harbour. *Circa* 1950. (Author's Collection).

the yard of Josiah Farrell in North Bay, La Poile. In the summer of that year, the 45-foot *Billard Brothers* was launched. The brothers fished the *Billard Brothers* until the 1950s when she was sold to the mainland. The final destiny of the *Billard Brothers* was in Prince Edward Island were she was beached as being of no further use.

The Loss of the Hilda

During the last several decades, navigational technology has advanced considerably, especially since the introduction of computers. The bridge of a modern day fishing boat consists of equipment such as radars, electronic charts, GPS, VHF telephones, satellite communications, autopilot, and depth sounders. These vessels are also being driven by powerful engines.

This of course was not the case in the days of skiffs and schooners when the navigational equipment consisted of a magnetic compass, a sounding lead, and a speed log. The only means of propulsion were sails until the late 1930s, and the steering systems were nothing more than a large wooden wheel rigged with rope and chain and exposed to the sea.

Even though the fishing boats of today have all the elegant equipment, things still can go wrong. Hence one can easily imagine the dangers faced by sailors eighty years ago when they were forced, in a blinding snowstorm, to navigate the entrance to some of the treacherous ports along the southwest coast .

In the spring of 1927, the skiffs of Isle aux Morts were fishing in the vicinity of Channel, Port aux Basques, just several miles west of their home port. However, instead of returning to their home in Isle aux Morts, they would berth in Channel overnight to be close to the fishing grounds the following morning.

After a hard week of fishing, and Easter week approaching, the fishermen decided it was time to go home and rest over the holiday season and spend time with their families. In the mid-afternoon of

Saturday, April 9, 1927, seven of the fishing skiffs from Isle aux Morts were preparing for the short voyage home.

One of the skiffs that made up the Isle aux Morts fleet was the *Hilda*, a typical 15-20-ton skiff that was used mainly on the southwest coast.

When Ephraim Harvey returned to port for his last trip, he was short one crew member because John Harvey had to leave the vessel because of sickness. John Harvey was replacing another crew member named Thomas MacDonald, who had gotten sick from Isle aux Morts as well, but MacDonald's health had improved and he decided to return to the *Hilda* after Easter.

However, things would change when Thomas found that his replacement had become ill. He immediately left Isle aux Morts and walked to Channel to rejoin the crew. For the trip home on the *Hilda*, the crew consisted of Ephraim Harvey, Thomas MacDonald, Alexander Hatcher, Thomas Harvey from Isle aux Morts, and Jerry Keeping from Burnt Islands.

At approximately 15:00, on Saturday, April 9, 1927, the seven skiffs set sail from Channel, Port aux Basques, for their home at Isle aux Morts, some six miles away. The weather consisted of light northeast winds and overcast skies.

Shortly after the skiffs departed Channel, the northeast wind began to increase, bringing with it blinding snow, leaving the visibility near zero. The northeast wind continued to increase, until it eventually reached gale force, and in doing so, blew down several telegraph poles and discontinuing all communications along the coast.

At 20:00, five of the skiffs had reached the port of Isle aux Morts. The two remaining skiffs were unreported

Thomas Harvey, shown here while sailing out of Gloucester as a doryman.
(Photo courtesy of Thomas H. Harvey).

and family members and residents began to worry. Some of the fear was relieved the next morning when the sixth skiff arrived home after seeking shelter in a small cove overnight.

The fate of the seventh skiff, which was the *Hilda*, was uncertain. There were no other ships in the area to conduct a search. The gulf ferry MV *Caribou* was delayed in Louisburg, Nova Scotia, due to high winds, and no other vessel could be reached because of the loss of communications.

Late the next day, the winds began to abate, and contacts were restored. Local residents began to search the area, along with the aid of the coastal boat. The result of the search included nothing more than several trawl buoys and some fishing gear that were found near Channel Head at the entrance to Channel Harbour, where the skiff *Hilda* had departed.

Because the crew had such a short distance to go, and in company of other fishing vessels, the fate of the *Hilda* must had been very sudden. It may have capsized quickly or ran aground with no time to abandon her.

Many of the local fishermen strongly feel that the *Hilda* went aground on a treacherous place along their journey named "Fox Roost Black Rock" when the visibility was reduced due to the snow. From Channel to Isle aux Morts, the course would have been nearly northeast, and for the simple reason, the trawl buoys and debris would have been carried back over the same area they had just come from.

In the hope of finding more wreckage, and maybe some of the bodies of the crew, fishermen and residents dragged an anchor on the bottom, but nothing else was ever found. The *Hilda* and her crew had become another mystery of the sea. Of the five fishermen lost on the *Hilda*, four of them were married with children. The only unmarried crew member was Alexander Hatcher.

There were rumours that some of the bodies were recovered months later and placed in the cemetery at Fox Roost, but there were no official records found to confirm this.

The Loss of the Vianna

In the early 1900s, the fishery along the south and southwest coast of Newfoundland had experienced a major decrease in cod catches. The result of such a decrease had a great effect and some of the fish firms even went into bankruptcy.

The firm of R. Moulton Limited was operating out of Burgeo at the time and was one of the firms that went into liquidation. As a result of the insolvency, The Burgeo and La Poile Export Company was formed.

The Burgeo and La Poile Export Company had businesses in several communities, but one of the largest operations was a whaling factory in the community of Burnt Islands on the southwest coast. Along with the factory, the firm owned and operated several skiffs which were crewed by local seaman and commanded by local captains, one being Captain John "Jack" Chaulk.

Jack Chaulk was a well-known fisherman and became a captain when he was still in his early twenties. At the age of twenty-six, he was in command of a fishing skiff and survived the infamous Southwest Coast Disaster in January 1925. He and his crew were in grave danger and had to abandon their vessel, but fortunately they were rescued by Captain Bill Durnford of Francois, who was also battered by the winter storm while fishing in the area. Captain Chaulk's skiff was driven out to sea and never seen again, but Captain Durnford and his crew, along with Captain Chaulk and his crew finally sought shelter in a small community several miles west of La Poile called West Point. They remained there until the weather improved.

With the lost of the skiff, the Burgeo and La Poile Export

Company immediately wanted a replacement for the prosperous young captain so they hired a carpenter from Burnt Islands named John Keeping to build another skiff. Consequently, in the spring of 1926, the 46-foot vessel *Vianna* was launched.

Now it was time for Captain Jack Chaulk and his crew to return to sea, but this time they would not be returning to the fishery. Instead they were hired by the owners of the *Vianna* to carry and pick up supplies from various ports along the coast.

The coasting trade went well for the crew of the *Vianna*, and in August of 1927, the *Vianna* and her crew had gone to the french islands of St. Pierre and Miqueon to pick up their cargo for ports back home. After the cargo was loaded, the vessel departed the french islands for her 110-nautical-mile journey back home.

On Thursday, August 24, 1927, the coastline and fishing grounds of Newfoundland were battered by high winds and seas from what was later known as the "August Gale." The "August Gales" had occurred years before and the results from such storms were devastating.

The August Gale of 1927 would be no different from that of the previous ones. The fishing ports of Nova Scotia were among the hardest hit when three of their large bankers from the port of Lunenburg and another from the port of Gloucester, were lost with all crew in the vicinity if Sable Island. In total nearly 200 men perished.

Back home in Newfoundland, schooners and skiffs had been reported as being driven ashore, partly damaged, losing crew members overboard, and some were overdue.

The exact time the *Vianna* departed the french islands will probably never be known, but what is fact is that on Thursday, August 24, when the storm hit the south and southwest coast area, the *Vianna* and her crew were right in the storm's path.

A day or so after the storm, residents of Burnt Islands discovered wreckage just west of their community near Hiscock's Point. It was later discovered as belonging to the *Vianna*.

Because the wreckage was found so close to home a day after the storm, it gave all indication that either the *Vianna* must have been

Captain James Chaulk and an unidentified sailor taken in Halifax several years before he was lost. (Author's Collection).

near home and waiting outside the port for the weather to improve, or they were attempting to enter the port when they met their fate.

Unfortunately, the wreckage was all that was found. There were never any bodies or other debris found of the *Vianna* apart from what was found shortly after the storm.

Captain Jack Chaulk had just gotten married shortly before he was lost. Mrs. Chaulk had also lost her father on the *Vianna*, Robert Herritt.

Several weeks after the disaster, Mrs. Chaulk gave birth to a boy whom she named John after his father. The crew lost on the *Vianna* were:

> Jack Chaulk, Burnt Islands
> Robert Herritt, Burnt Islands
> John P. Keeping, Burnt Islands
> Thomas Keeping, Burnt Islands
> Freeman Organ, Burnt Islands
> George Strickland, East Bay, La Poile

The Loss of Three Rose Blanche Fishermen

In the late 1920s and the early 1930s, many of the Newfoundland outports were beginning to see the first of what was later known as the Great Depression. These were difficult time for many families, still men and women alike did everything they could to provide for their loved ones.

In the hope of providing a better life for their families in a time of such an economic downturn, many fishermen along the southwest coast of Newfoundland left home to search for work in the fishing industry. Some went to such ports as Halifax and Lunenburg, Nova Scotia, and some went as far Gloucester and Boston, Massachusetts. In these places, the fleets were larger and the economy was a little more prosperous.

Some of the fishermen did find berths on schooners and managed to provide a better life for their families. However, there were others who met their fate on the very schooners they had hoped would better their lives.

In 1929, William Hardy was a young and energetic twenty-year-old fisherman who wanted to pursue a career in the bank fishery. To fulfill his career, he joined the many Newfoundland fishermen before him and left home for the famous port of Lunenburg, to look for a berth on board a banking schooner. It would not be long before William would be in luck, and shortly after arriving in Lunenburg, he secured a berth aboard the MV *Mahaska*, a 106-foot 97-ton schooner built in Lunenburg in 1922.

On March 11, 1929 the *Mahaska* departed Lunenburg under the command of Captain Dylan Fleet who was in command for the first time. The vessel carried eight dories and nineteen men. They were:

Dylan Fleet	Captain	Port Blandford, NS
Angus Hiltz	Cook	Martin's Point, NS
Simeon Cleveland	Throater	Bay's Water, NS
Thomas Hubley	Doryman	Bay's Water, NS
Mathers Fleet	Doryman	Port Blandford, NS
John Fleet	Doryman	Port Blandford, NS
Stephen Grandy	Doryman	Lunenburg, NS
Mahion Berringer	Doryman	Lunenburg, NS
Fred Zinck	Doryman	Rose Bay, NS
Perry Greek	Doryman	Blue Rocks, NS
Roderick Hamm	Doryman	Chester, NS
Warren Levy	Doryman	First South, NS
Burton Levy	Doryman	First South, NS
Alphonse Antle	Doryman	Fox Cove, NS
Edward Smith	Doryman	Fox Cove, NS
William Hardy	Doryman	Rose Blanche, NL
Cecil Petro	Doryman	New Harbour, NL
Leo Hackett	Doryman	English Harbour West, NL
John Hackett	Doryman	English Harbour West, NL

The fishing grounds for this particular voyage were the Western Banks some 100 miles southeast of Halifax.

By the later part of March, the voyage was near completion. On the morning of March 22, 1929, the crew had returned to the schooner after a day of fishing. Shortly after their return, the crew were suddenly shaken and surprised by the noise of cracking and breaking wood. The *Mahaska* had been struck by another vessel and the *Mahaska*'s crew had just enough time to abandon the schooner as she sank beneath their feet.

The vessel that had struck the *Mahaska* was the MV *Remy*

Chouinard, a steel trawler under the command of Captain Glatre and owned by *Societe Les Terreneuves* of Port de Granville, France. At the time of the collision, she was under charter by a Nova Scotia firm and her agent was James Fraser, also from Nova Scotia.

The *Remy Chouinard* began to pick up the survivors of the doomed schooner at once, but as time progressed, the crew's fears became reality when they discovered that two of the crew members, William Hardy and John Fleet were missing. They searched the area hoping to find them but they were unsuccessful. The bodies of William Hardy and John Fleet were never recovered.

ARCHIBALD PARSONS

Like William Hardy, Archibald Parsons had grown up in Rose Blanche during the same era. When Archibald was a young lad, he would often see the large Lunenburg bankers visit the port during the times when they were participating in the thriving winter fishery on the Western Shore.

In the early 1930s, Archibald Parsons decided to leave his home behind in the hope of pursuing a career aboard one of the large banking schooners in one of the most prosperous fishing ports on the east coast, Lunenburg, Nova Scotia. It was not long before Archibalds was in luck, and shortly after arriving in Lunenburg, he secured a berth on one of the largest banking schooners in the Lunenburg fleet, the MV *Marguerite B. Tanner.*

The *Marguerite B. Tanner* was typical of a Lunenburg banker, being built there by the famous shipbuilders Smith and Ruhland. The 121-foot twelve-dory banker was owned and operated by a well respected and successful captain named Angus Tanner. The schooner was well-known to Newfoundland seamen and oftentimes carried Newfoundland crew.

In late February 1931, the *Marguerite B. Tanner* and her crew had left Lunenburg for a fresh fishing trip on the grounds of Banquero Bank, some 200 nautical miles east of Lunenburg. The

MV *Marguerite B. Tanner* berthed in a Newfoundland outport.
(Maritime History Archives, Captain Harry Stone Collection).

morning of February 25, 1931, started out as nothing more than a typical day on the fishing grounds. The skies were clear with light winds. The dories were lowered over the side and the fishing began. The trawl was set out and the men returned to the schooner for a short lunch before retrieving their trawl.

After a short while aboard, and a hearty meal from the cook, the fishermen boarded their dories and began to row back to their keg. Once there, they immediately began to retrieve their trawl. The weather still consisted of light winds, smooth seas, and light snow flurries.

Shortly after the dories began to retrieve their trawl, one occupant of the dories made a gruesome discovery when they came upon another one of their dories that was swamped and her crew nowhere to be seen. The fisherman notified the other dories and went back to notify Captain Tanner at once. All of the other dories rushed to the scene in the hope of finding their shipmates. The crew had done the best they could in the search, yet the occupants of the dory were lost.

How and why the dory capsized was a mystery to the crew. It is known that they had just started hauling their trawl, therefore the dory would not have been overloaded. The weather conditions were good, and a Lunenburg dory could have certainly stood much more.

The crew of the *Marguerite B. Tanner* searched for hours, and unfortunately they found nothing. The bodies of Archibald Parsons and Alton Hiltz, both only twenty-eight, were never recovered. Late that evening, Captain Tanner set course for North Sydney, with the flag at half-mast to display the loss of two of their seamen.

HENRY BEST

Henry Best was also born in Rose Blanche to George and Mary Best on June 1, 1910. Henry was the second youngest. He also had one older brother John, a younger brother William, and two younger sisters, but unfortunately the three youngest siblings died as infants. Mary Best passed away, leaving George to care for Henry and John.

Not long after, George Best met a young lady from Burgeo named Caroline Porter. Caroline was a young widow with three children. George and Caroline later married and the couple had two children, Garland born February 13, 1920, and Joseph born August 31, 1923.

By the 1920s, when things seemed to finally settle down for the Best family, there came the beginnings of one of the toughest times in Newfoundland, the Great Depression. Henry and his siblings along with both his father and stepmother had seen enough hard times. In the beginning of the Great Depression, many Newfoundlanders went to the mainland to find work, and although Henry was only a young lad, he decided to do the same.

Henry's first stop, like many people from the southwest coast of

Newfoundland was the port of North Sydney, a busy fishing port on Cape Breton Island. Once at North Sydney, Henry found some work in the fishery, but Cape Breton too was feeling the effects of the Depression and often times Henry would be left out of work.

During those particular times, Henry participated in the sport of boxing. At the time, Henry was a tall and well-built young man in his twenties. Consequently, he entered local boxing contests to earn a little extra money, and he often won.

After a short while in North Sydney, Henry met a young lady named Martha Vallis, from English Harbour, Fortune Bay, on the south coast of Newfoundland. Within no time a romance sparked, and a little while later, the two were married.

Shortly after they were married, Henry and his young bride decided to leave North Sydney and look for a future somewhere else. Consequently they decided to go to the famous fishing port of Lunenburg.

By now the Depression was nearing an end and banking

Henry Best. (Photo courtesy of Annabella King).

fleets in the port of Lunenburg were beginning to thrive from the new demand for fresh fish.

After Henry and his wife resettled to Lunenburg, the couple had five children, but two of them died as infants. Although it was tough times for the family, it was nothing new to Henry. He had gone through similar grief once before, when as a boy, his own two siblings died very young.

After several years, Henry had become a well-respected fisherman and got along great with his shipmates. He went on to work aboard some of the largest banking schooners that sailed out of Lunenburg.

In the spring of 1942, Henry joined the crew of the MV *Alcala*, a 121-foot twelve-dory banker, which he fished on for the remainder of the season. The next year, he was offered a berth aboard the MV *Flora Alberta*.

The *Flora Alberta* was another of the twelve-dory bankers. She was launched from the Smith & Rhuland Yard in Lunenburg just two years before. Securing a berth aboard the *Flora Alberta* was not exactly easy for the simple fact that the schooner was under the command of Captain Guy Tanner, one of the most successful captains that ever sailed the Lunenburg banker fleet.

In April 1943, the *Flora Alberta* departed Lunenburg for the first fresh fish trip of the year. Her destination was the fishing grounds some 100 miles south of Halifax.

The beginning of the trip was successful, and on the evening of April 20, 1943, the dories were taken aboard and the crew prepared for supper. After the fish was put away and supper finished, the crew retired in their bunks for the night.

Shortly before midnight, the schooner was experiencing heavy fog, and the watch on deck carried out his job with constant vigilance. Henry Best was one of them.

Although the crew were looking and listening cautiously, they were still unfortunate, as the bow of a merchant ship struck the *Flora Alberta* at amidships. She sank immediately.

Some of the crew managed to jump overboard and cling to the

MV *Fanad Head* in the United Kingdom. (Photo courtesy of Shipsearch Marine).

wreckage. The others who were sleeping down below were not so fortunate. Of the crew of twenty-eight, only seven survived. Henry who was making up part of the watch at the time of the collision, was not one of the fortunate ones. Not only was he the only one in the watch to lose his life, his body was never found. As mentioned before, Henry was a strong and able young man, and also a very good swimmer, so what could have gone wrong?

Back home in Lunenburg, and the surrounding area, many wives were left widows, and many children were left fatherless. Henry left a wife and three children at the time, the oldest being six and the youngest just two. Although the tragedy took its toll on the families, they found the strength and determination to carry on with their lives.

Some sixteen years after the collision in 1959, Henry's youngest daughter Annabella, who had very few memories of her father, decided to enroll in a nursing program in Halifax. After three years of hard work and determination, Annabella successfully completed her nursing courses and prepared for the night of the graduation.

In May of 1962, Annabella and her roommate were waiting in their room at the residence complex preparing for the big event. The only phone in the building was located in the hallway for everyone's use.

Shortly before Annabella and her friend were leaving their room to attend the graduation ceremony, the phone rang. Annabella's roommate ran to answer the phone. Moments later, she called Annabella's name telling her that the phone call was for her. Annabella ran to get the call, hoping it was someone to congratulate her on her three years of hard work.

In his congratulations, the voice at the other end sounded older, and he told Annabella that he was very proud of her accomplishment, and since she was a child, he had watched over her. The voice had somewhat startled Annabella. When the gentleman at the other end of the phone line was finished speaking, Annabella asked who was speaking. The gentleman said he was unable to tell her saying that by giving his name he would probably bring more harm than good. He then hung up.

Who was the gentleman at the other end of the phone line? Annabella never did any travelling so it was not anyone she had met. Several days later she returned home and told he mother of her experience. Her mother had no idea who the man could have been, but Annabella often wondered if the voice could have been that of her father Henry. Did Henry survive the collision of the *Flora Alberta* and was later rescued, then maybe taken to a foreign port? Annabella's mother remarried after the collision of the *Flora Alberta*. Maybe Henry was rescued, and by the time he returned to Canada, his wife was remarried and he did not want to trouble the lives of his former wife and children.

Annabella never heard from him again. She later married Winston King and worked her whole career as a nurse until she retired.

Also lost on the *Flora Alberta* was another fisherman from the southwest coast named Wesley Anderson. Wesley was born and raised in Petites, just several miles east of Rose Blanche. Wesley first got introduced to the Lunenburg schooner fleet by making a trip with his brother-in-law Griffon. Griffon was also from Petites, but had sailed with the Lunenburg banking fleet many times before.

Wesley like Henry, went to Lunenburg in the hope of a better future during the days of the Great Depression. Shortly after arriving

Inez and Wesley Anderson on their wedding day in 1929.
(Photo courtesy of Marion Robar).

in Lunenburg, Wesley met and married Inez Philpott of Upper La Have and the couple had three children.

On February 21, 1941, Inez passed away at the age of twenty-nine and Wesley was left with three children to care for. Inez's family immediately helped Wesley raise the young family. Although times were tough for Wesley, he continued to fish on the large Lunenburg bankers to help support his three children. When he was offered a berth with one of the Lunenburg highliners on the *Flora Alberta*, he gladly took it.

Unfortunately, Wesley Anderson, like Henry Best, who came to Lunenburg seeking a better life, and who tried so hard to provide the best for his family, met his fate aboard the *Flora Alberta* on that terrible night. The body of Wesley Anderson like that of Henry Best was never recovered.

The MV *Frances Geraldine*, a twelve-dory Lunenburg Banker similiar to the MV *Flora Alberta*.
(Photo courtesy of Shipsearch Marine).

West Point Tragedy

If one was to sit and compare the childhood memories of someone from a large suburb and the childhood memories of a person from a Newfoundland outport, the differences would be considerable to say the least. For children in rural and outport Newfoundland, as soon as boys and girls were old enough to work, they would help their parents with everyday chores.

In 1932, Henry Strickland and his wife made a happy couple in the Newfoundland community of West Point, located on the southwest coast. In the spring of that year, Henry, like many local fishermen, was preparing his fishing gear for the upcoming annual salmon run, one of the more prosperous times of year along the Newfoundland shore.

April 14, 1932, started as a typical spring day for the Strickland family. It was somewhat warm, and in the afternoon, Henry was working away in his shed carrying out repairs to his nets.

Henry and his wife had three children: two daughters and one son. Like any child, Henry's son John Robert had enough of playing inside and wanted to explore outdoors, particularly in the shed where his father was.

John Robert's mother agreed to let him visit his father and dressed the boy at once. The child left the house and made his way toward the shed where his father was working. Because Henry's shed was only several hundred yards from his house, his wife thought her son would reach his father without incident, but unfortunately she was wrong.

Henry continued to work away at his nets, and after a short while, he noticed that he dadn't heard anything from his son. Immediately, Henry began to call the boy's name. John Robert was nowhere to be heard or seen. Several other residents heard Henry calling out to the boy and went to see what was wrong.

In no time, the whole community of West Point was calling and looking for John Robert. The residents searched all the stores, stages, and even boats. Where could a five-year-old boy have disappeared so suddenly?

The afternoon turned to night and the search was given up. Early the next morning, the residents searched the area again. In the very area where the child went missing, a small stream flows to the sea, and because of the previous heavy rain, the water level was above normal. With this in mind, the residents searched the shoreline around the community and nearby islands. Still there was no luck.

After days of searching, the family had to face the fact that the boy was gone. They knew that if the child went astray in some adjacent wooded area, he would be unable to survive on his own at such a young age. For the Strickland family, life had to continue. One can only wonder how a family can pull through such a calamity.

Two weeks after the tragedy, a report came that a man while

West Point, showing the location where Henry Strickland lived and where John Robert went missing. (Author's Collection).

walking on a beach near Codroy, some sixty miles away on the west coast of Newfoundland, had found the body of a child that was partly discomposed. The body was taken to Port aux Basques, and immediately the family members of John Robert Strickland went to see the remains. An older sister of the young boy positively identified the body as that of her baby brother.

Now that they had some sort of closure, many wondered how the body of the child escaped the closely searched harbour and shoreline of West Point and drifted on a beach near Codroy. To many it may have seemed a mystery, but in actual fact, it's not.

The course the child's body had taken was due mostly to the effect of the current, then the wind. Ocean currents are categorized in two different types; drift currents and stream currents. Drift currents mostly occur in the open ocean and are caused by wind blowing in the same direction for lengthy periods of time, causing the water to move in the same direction. Stream currents, on the other hand, are caused by things such as a change in water level, change in water density, and the coastline characteristics.

Days preceding the boy's tragedy, the weather consisted of southeast and easterly winds along with rain. The rain of course, had caused the water level in the creeks and rivers to rise.

The current along the shoreline to the westward of the Avalon Peninsula and onward to the south and southwest coast would be a stream current, which flows to the westward until the entrance of the Cabot Strait, where the direction changes more northerly, following again the general outline of the coast.

In times after heavy rain, the volume of water flowing out of the rivers into bays and inlets increases, thus causing the current flowing to the seaward to increase as well. When this seaward flow meets the westward current from the Avalon, they combine into one current with a stronger rate.

If the rain and wind had not caused the increase in the current, it was most likely that the body of John Robert Strickland would have been carried further out in the vast ocean, and never discovered. Then, if the heavy rain never occurred, then the water level in the little river by his home in West Point would not have been so high, and the child would probably not have drowned.

After the body was identified, it was prepared for burial in a small wooden coffin and laid to rest in the United cemetery in Channel.

The Strickland Family Tragedies

The community of Rose Blanche, on the southwest coast of Newfoundland is home for many fishermen and their families. Some common family names in the area include Hatcher, Parsons, Hardy, Herritt, and Strickland.

As with the others, Robert and Annie Strickland's family was well-known and respected. They were a hard-working fishing family who learned the necessary skills for fishing from one another. Unfortunately, the family was not only recognized for their hard work and dedication, but they were also known for the hardships they endured and the tragedies they experienced.

Robert and Annie had seven children; five sons and two daughters. Of the five sons, four of them, John, George, Henry, and Chesley became fishermen and fished together in a 44-foot skiff named the *Phoebe A.* The oldest, John, was in command.

The four brothers worked hard together on the *Phoebe A.*, and the morning of December 21, 1917, was to be a typical trip to the fishing grounds on Rose Blanche Bank. Shortly after the brothers arrived on the grounds, the area was swiped by northeasterly wind, and the brothers were unable to make it back to their home port. The *Phoebe A.* and her crew began to battle high winds and subsequent high seas. Back at home, their father knew something was wrong as he anxiously waited to see his sons.

The bad weather continued for days and no word was heard from the vessel or her crew. The family had no way of knowing if the crew managed to seek shelter along the shore because the high winds had interrupted the communications by damaging the telegraph lines.

Now the family could do only one thing, and that was to wait for news whether good or bad.

However, the family was in luck. Although the crew were young, they had acquired enough skill to keep their sturdy craft afloat. They eventually made landfall to the east at Burgeo. Although they barely escaped their ordeal and left their families spirits shaken, they continued to work in the fishing industry.

Shortly after this incident, George took command of the 62-foot banking schooner *Cora B. Rose*, which he commanded until 1927. Although George was in command of a banking schooner, he still dreamed of owning his own boat. As a result, in 1927, he placed an order at North Bay, La Poile, to master boat builder Josiah Farrell. In 1928, his dream came true when he became the proud owner of the 45-foot *Danny Catherine*.

For George and his new bride Catherine, life could not have been better. He was a successful fisherman with a new boat, a wonder-

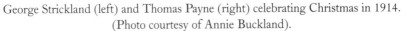

George Strickland (left) and Thomas Payne (right) celebrating Christmas in 1914. (Photo courtesy of Annie Buckland).

ful wife, and eight children, named Maud, Lewis, Maria, Danny, Annie, Wilfred, George, and Roy.

Life continued as normal, and in March of 1935, the couple added another member to their family, a baby girl named Catherine, totalling the children to nine. Unfortunately, just days after giving birth to their daughter, the young mother became ill with pneumonia. She was unable to overcome the illness, and on March 26, 1935, she passed away at the age of thirty-nine.

George was devastated by the loss of his wife. He also found himself in a terrible situation. He was alone with nine children to care for, ranging from a few weeks old to sixteen years. He wanted to provide the best possible life for his children, and as a result, he hired a female helper from Fortune Bay named Miss Green.

Although times were tough, Miss Green and George's oldest daughter Maud, cared for the children. However, four months after his wife passed away, George was faced with tragedy again when his youngest daughter Catherine died on July 30, 1935. Again George and his family were devastated, but somehow found the strength and courage to continue on.

George continued to fish on the *Danny Catherine* and became quite successful. In the summer of 1943, George returned home to Rose Blanche, after a summer of swordfishing out of Glace Bay, Nova Scotia. He had a total catch of fifty-nine swordfish—a fine summer's catch to say the least. However, again bad news awaited his return.

Once he arrived in Glace Bay, he was informed that his brother John had passed away at the North Sydney hospital. Shortly after hearing the news, George unloaded his swordfish and returned home to Rose Blanche to attend the funeral.

A week after the passing of his brother, George decided to make his annual run to Nova Scotia to pick up a load of coal and supplies for the upcoming winter. In late September, George and his two sons Lewis and Dan, departed Rose Blanche for North Sydney. Unfortunately, shortly after departing, George became ill, so Lewis decided to take his father to the nearest doctor in Neil's Harbour, Nova Scotia.

Upon their arrival, they discovered, to their dismay, that the doctor had left town just hours earlier. George Strickland was unable to make it to any other medical facility and he passed away the very same night with spinal meningitis, just one week after he attended his brother's funeral. George Strickland's body was returned to Rose Blanche for burial.

The Strickland family grieved over the tragedy. Now the remaining children were forced to go on, without a mother or father. Fortunately for the children, their parents had taught them good values and work ethics during their short years together. George's three sons were left to fish the *Danny Catherine* and support the family.

However, it would not be long before illness would plague the family yet again. This time, in the winter of 1945, seventeen-year-old Wilfred became ill, just two years short of the passing of his father. He was experiencing severe pain in his right side that would not go away. Wilfred, on several occasions, visited the local doctor, but the doctor had few answers or solutions. As the pain continued, Wilfred decided to visit another local doctor who diagnosed him with appendicitis. The doctor also suggested that he admit himself at St. Elizabeth Hospital in Nova Scotia to have his appendix removed, as the operation could not be carried out back home.

Wilfred followed the doctor's instructions. However, when he arrived at the hospital in Glace Bay, he received unexpected news. The doctors told him that the operation could not be conducted because his appendix had ruptured.

The doctors treated Wilfred as best as they could and extended his life for another three months. During the three months, the young man was given large doses of Penicillin—the newest drug on the market at that time. Wilfred's suffering finally came to an end when he passed away on July 12, 1945. The family was again griefstricken.

Once again, the Strickland family picked up the pieces and moved on with what they had. Now, twenty-one-year-old Danny was in command of the *Danny Catherine* and he did everything he could to help his siblings.

On the morning of April 19, 1946, the *Danny Catherine* and her

Wilfred Strickland and Ethel Dollimount at Rose Blanche in 1943.
(Photo courtesy of Annie Buckland).

crew set sail for the fishing grounds east of Rose Blanche, near Seal Islands. Besides Danny, the crew consisted of his brother Lewis, Joseph Best, and Roland Loder. They were fishing only one dory, so Joseph and Danny remained aboard the skiff while the others hauled

the trawl. The day consisted of high winds and increasing seas, but nothing the young fishermen were not accustomed to.

Shortly before lunch, Danny was making his way to the main deck from the forecastle. As he approached the deck through the passageway, the sea and wind had caused the boat to roll, resulting in Danny being hit by the boom and was knocked overboard. Joseph was aft and saw the incident take place. He quickly turned the skiff around in the hope of retrieving him. To his distress, Danny was nowhere to be found.

The crew searched the waters for hours, but found nothing. The blow from the boom must have knocked him unconscious, rendering him defenceless in the cold water. His body was never recovered. At the time of his death, he was a month away from his twenty-second birthday.

With the awful loss of Danny, the *Danny Catherine*'s career ended and she was left moored at Rose Blanche. Lewis and the other brothers went elsewhere to work.

Maud who was the oldest child, witnessed every moment of hardship endured by her family. She had married a well-known hardworking respectable fisherman from Rose Blanche named Alexander 'Sandy' Hatcher. They had two daughters and two sons.

Maud was a dedicated church attendant. Hence, on the evening of June 23, 1968, Maud and her youngest daughter Cathy Ann were dressed to attend the evening service. Shortly after leaving the house, they encountered several dogs in the pathway leading to the church. Fearing for the safety of her child Maud decided it would be best to return home.

Shortly before they entered the house, Maud and Cathy Ann saw Sandy chatting with some of the local fishermen. Cathy Ann wanted to remain outside with her father. Maud agreed, as she knew her husband would soon be retiring for the night.

Sandy seemed to linger outside a little longer on this particular evening and Maud decided it was time for Cathy Ann to come inside. She went outside to tell her husband it was time for Cathy Ann to come back indoors. Maud called to Cathy Ann, but the call was not answered. Maud then alerted Sandy to see if he had seen her. His reply was that he last saw her playing with one of her friends some time ago. Sandy suddenly became startled because he had seen Cathy Ann going towards the house and consequently thought she was inside.

Immediately they grew frantic and feared the worst. Everyone began to search, but there weren't many places for her to wander. Sandy decided to check a nearby drinking well. When he arrived at the place, he was horrified when he saw the body of his daughter at the bottom. Attempts were made to revive the child as she was rushed to the hospital in Channel-Port aux Basques. Unfortunately it was too late. The body of three-and-a-half-year-old Cathy Ann Hatcher was laid to rest in the local cemetery a few days later.

Cathy Ann Hatcher aged three. (Photo courtesy of Annie Buckland).

Maud and Sandy mourned the loss of their child for months and some say they never really recovered from it. Maud and her family had endured far more than their share of tragedies over the years. However, their hardships were still not over.

Maud's oldest daughter Marie, had married a fisherman from Rose Blanche named Gerald Wagg. Gerald was the youngest of three children. He had lost his father at three years of age. His father was a crew member on board the *Julia A. Anderson.* She was lost with all crew en route from Harbour Breton to Port aux Basques in April 1936.

On the morning of October 1, 1984, Gerald and several friends from Rose Blanche were hunting seabirds in the vicinity of Couteau Bay, some thirty miles east of Rose Blanche. Gerald did not survive the return trip home. He drowned while bird hunting and his body was never found. He was fifty-two years old at the time with two children and a grandchild.

Most parents don't expect to outlive their children, however, Maud did in 1995 when she lost her son Winston to cancer. Needless to say, the Strickland family had experienced many hardships. Maud became ill and passed away in November 2001, at the age of eighty-three. Her sister Maria passed away in 1995, at the age of seventy-four. The remainder of the family retired to different locations: Lewis resides in Glace Bay, Nova Scotia; Roy resides in Bellevue, Ontario, George in St. John's, Newfoundland; and Annie in Harbour Le Cou, Newfoundland. Their story proves that life goes on and that we don't know our own strength until it's tested time and time again.

Gerald Wagg holding daughter Michelle, wife Marie, and daughter Geraldine in 1972. (Photo courtesy of Marie Wagg).

The Loss of the Julia A. Anderson

Early one fall morning in 1935, Rose Blanche residents William 'Bill' Wagg and Eli Chislett departed Rose Blanche on a routine bird hunting trip along the shoreline. The sky was overcast with light easterly winds. It was one of the better weather forecasts for hunting seabirds.

Shortly after they departed, the men had noticed a derelict schooner to the west of the entrance to Rose Blanche harbour. It was located close to the shoreline near an area known as White Shoal. Both Bill and Eli, being experience hunters and fishermen, knew the area well, and realized immediately that something wasn't right.

From where the men were located, it appeared that the schooner was still afloat and seaworthy, but not moving. They knew that the easterly wind would increase later in the day, and that White Shoals was not a good place to be. Their knowledge told them that the easterly wind would gradually cause the sea in the area to build and the schooner would be driven onto the rocks and beaten to pieces. With this in mind, they decided to row towards the schooner to check it out further.

Their investigation revealed that the schooner was the MV *Julia A. Anderson*, under command of Captain Alexander Chiasson from Channel, just eighteen miles to the westward. The schooner was sailing along the coastline on a route-coasting run when it was driven into to the treacherous area and having trouble getting clear.

Immediately, Bill Wagg and Eli Chislett lent a helping hand to the captain and the crew, but getting the schooner in safer water was not a easy task. However, after a day of hard work, they finally succeeded.

By the time the schooner and her crew were finally safe, it was late in the day and near dusk. The captain felt that it wouldn't be safe for Eli and Bill to return to Rose Blanche that night, so he took the hunters aboard until daybreak. Early the next morning, Captain Chiasson berthed the *Julia A. Anderson* at the dock in Rose Blanche, but before he bade Eli and Bill farewell, he wanted to repay the gentlemen for their comradeship. As a result, he offered the two gentleman a berth on the schooner the next spring when the coasting season started. Most people who knew Captain Alex Chiasson, also known as 'Saxie,' knew he was a well-respected man, a man of his word.

Early the next spring, Captain Chaission stood true to his word and arrived in Rose Blanche to fulfill the promise he made almost six months before. Once arriving in Rose Blanche, only Bill Wagg joined the crew of the *Julia A. Anderson* for the coasting season. Eli Chislett

and his two brothers normally fished with their father who had just taken command of a new fishing skiff named the *Brenda Chislett*.

The *Julia A. Anderson* soon departed Rose Blanche to commence her first coasting trip of the year. In early April, the vessel proceeded to the south coast community of Harbour Breton to load fish salt, which was to be delivered to the firm of E. Pike at Channel.

On April 6, 1936, the

William Wagg aged twenty.
(Photo courtesy of Athena Wagg Buckland).

vessel was loaded and departed the Harvey Dock in Harbour Breton. Several other vessels departed the same time, but had other destinations.

On Tuesday, April 7, the *Julia A. Anderson* was reported as being sighted by another schooner in the vicinity of New Harbour, just east of Ramea. At the time, she was stopped in the water and carrying out engine repairs. The next day, on Wednesday, April 8, the south and southwest coast of Newfoundland was hit by a late winter storm that continued on into the next day.

At Burgeo, the storm had already claimed the lives of Frank Strickland and his two sons. They were lost when their dory capsized while retrieving a herring net.

The crew of a fishing skiff from Otter's Point barely escaped misfortune as well when they were battered by the storm that carried away all of vessel's canvas. The crew managed to keep the skiff afloat until they finally made landfall on the island of St. Pierre. The coasting schooner *Sentia*, under command of Captain Matt Pink of Harbour Le Cou, was also battered by the same storm. It had tremendous difficulty along the southwest cost while en route from St. John's to her home port of Harbour Le Cou.

The storm continued to ravage on for two days, and boats were being driven ashore and lost all along the Newfoundland coast. Family members of the crew of the *Julia A. Anderson* were now beginning to worry because no one had heard from them in several days. The only news was that she had been seen the previous day.

After several days, there was still no sign of the schooner and her crew. The 56-foot vessel schooner was very stable and seaworthy. She had been built in Channel just eleven years before and Captain Chiasson always kept the schooner in good shape.

More days passed, with still no sign of the schooner and her crew, the families feared the worst. The customs cutter MV *Shulamite* searched the area around St. Paul's and the Cabot Strait, while the passenger ship SS *Kyle* searched the south and southwest coast. None of the vessels turned up anything.

On Wednesday, April 15, one week after the *Julia A. Anderson* was last seen, another schooner named the MV *Alice & Adelaide*, under command of Captain Roberts was making a routine voyage along the south coast en route to Placentia. When the *Alice & Adelaide* was passing some thirty-six miles west of St. Pierre, the crew came upon two spars approximately fifty feet in length and fish crates marked JE. Although the initials would have not exactly matched the name, many believe that the wreckage belonged to the missing schooner.

One such theory on the final destiny of the schooner and her crew was compared to similar fates of vessels that had been caught in storms laden with salt. It is thought that after high winds and seas battered the vessel for several days, the salt deteriorated the packing in the seams, and the battering from the storm only contributed to the ingress of water, faster than the pumps could discharge. Also the suction for the pumps being in the bilge was most likely plugged from the salt. Because the schooner was heavily laden, she would have sunk fast and the mast and rigging would have broken loose as it would have been its most vulnerable structure. The spars spotted by the schooner were indeed very similar to the size that *Julia A. Anderson* would have carried.

Again the theory is only one of many that may have caused the loss of the schooner and her crew. At the time of her disappearance she carried a crew of four. They consisted of:

Alexander Chiasson, aged sixty, Channel
Morgan Roberts, Burgeo
William" Bill" Wagg, aged twenty-nine, Rose Blanche
Alexander Hatcher, Burgeo

The Wreck of the Mizpah

November 6, 1937, was planned to be a special day for the residents and children of Grand Bruit, on the southwest coast of Newfoundland. It was a day when Bishop Philip Abraham was to visit the community to carry out confirmation services to the local children.

To make sure everything and everyone was prepared for the special event, the Church of England rector, Reverend Joseph Ayris, visited the community in late October, to make sure everything was in place. Grand Bruit, like the remainder of the communities, was experiencing the days of the Great Depression. However, both the Anglican and United Church were decorated to their highest extent.

Joining Bishop Philip Abraham, at Grand Bruit for the ceremony, was the head of the United Church, Reverend Oliver Jackson. A native of Wales, England, Reverend Jackson was the superintendent of the missions with the United Church of Newfoundland. He arrived in West Point in early November, where he stayed with a local student minister named Reverend Wallace Harris of New Chelsea, Trinity Bay.

Reverend Wallace Harris, lived aboard a small boat named the MV *Mizpah* at West Point, just several miles to the west of Grand Bruit. The *Mizpah* was thirty feet in length and powered by a small gas engine and also fitted with several small sails. She had been built at North Bay, La Poile, by Albert Strickland several years before.

On Monday morning, November 3, 1937, Reverend Oliver Jackson and Reverend Wallace Harris prepared the *Mizpah* for its journey to Grand Bruit. But before they visited Grand Bruit, they were to visit the communities of La Poile and North Bay along the way to conduct services there as well.

The weather that Monday morning was not exactly hospitable, with a southeast wind and a sea running. However, the men decided to make the trip anyway. The main entrance to West Point was somewhat treacherous, so the two gentlemen had to pass further to the west around Shoe Island. Unfortunately, while the *Mizpah* was just abeam of Shoe Island, her engine began to develop trouble, and shortly after, it failed completely. Now the ministers found themselves in a distressing situation.

Although the *Mizpah* was equipped with sails, there would not have been enough time to rig the sails and get the *Mizpah* under control as the vessel and her crew were already in prudent danger. In a matter of minutes, the *Mizpah* went ashore and was smashed to pieces.

The men on shore watched in horror, and quickly went to the aid of the ministers. With the horrendous weather conditions, their aid was sluggish. When a local resident did arrive on the scene, it was already too late. Lying face down in the water was the body of twenty-eight-year-old Reverend Wallace Harris. They then searched the area for the body of Reverend Oliver Jackson, but it was nowhere to be found.

Early the next morning, the residents searched the shoreline again, and shortly after, the body of Reverent Oliver Jackson was discovered in a nearby cove not far from were the tragedy occurred. Both of the bodies were first taken to West Point. Later, the body of Reverend Olive Jackson was forwarded to St. John's, and the body of Reverend Wallace Harris was sent to his home in New Chelsea, Trinity Bay, where they were buried.

Several days later, after the winds had blown out of the north, and the seas had abated, local residents found money, knives, and other items from the *Mizpah*. They also found the shaft and coupling to the engine. The coupling had been broken from the shaft, which most likely caused the trouble the two ministers experienced with the engine.

The battered pieces of the *Mizpah* remained on the shoreline for years. However, the nameplate was erected over the door in the Oliver Jackson Memorial Hall in Western Bay, Newfoundland.

The night of the tragedy, Reverend Ayris held a memorial service in the Anglican Church in memory of the two men. On the following Sunday, a local lay reader in Grand Bruit, named John Robert Billard,

Top: Pointing from the wreck of the *Mizpah* to where it went aground. (Photo courtesy of United Church Archives, Newfoundland and Labrador Conference, Rev. H. M. Dawe fonds, 2.10.61).

Left: Robert Strickland, who found Rev. Jackson's body the morning after the tragedy, points to where the body was found. (Photo courtesy of United Church Archives, Newfoundland and Labrador Conference, Rev. H. M. Dawe fonds, 2.10.52).

held a similar memorial service in the United Church at Grand Bruit.

As for the confirmation, it still went ahead with Bishop Philip Abraham. He arrived in Grand Bruit on time by a fishing schooner from Burgeo named the *Alice M. Nash*.

Right: Wreckage of the *Mizpah*. (Photo courtesy of United Church Archives, Newfoundland and Labrador Conference, Rev. H. M. Dawe fonds, 2.10.60).

Medals of Bravery

Oftentimes, many fishermen and seafarers have witnessed their shipmates and comrades become victims of the sea. Most often, these incidents were brought on by weather conditions, and hence encumbering assistance. Yet, there were times when people have shown exceptional strength and courage at attempting to save lives.

On January 6, 1937, George Thomas of North Sydney, formerly of Harbour Le Cou, Newfoundland, set sail from the port of North Sydney, to the fishing grounds on the east side of Cape Breton in the vicinity of Ingonish. The crew on that January morning consisted of his two sons, Pervical and Samuel, Levi Hardy, and William Buffett of North Sydney (formerly of Rose Blanche), and William Munden of Petites, Newfoundland.

Captain Thomas was in command of the 43-foot, 20-ton skiff named the MV *Percy F. Russell*, which carried two dories. William Munden and Levi Hardy occupied the first dory while William Buffett and Percvial Thomas occupied the other. Samuel Thomas remained on the skiff to assist his father.

Shortly after arriving on the fishing grounds, Captain Thomas ordered the dories lowered. The wind was light and the seas were calm.

Once their dories were on the water, the fishermen began to set their trawl. Once the trawl was set, the dories returned to the skiff so

MV *Percy F. Russell* moored in Port Bickerton
Harbour in the 1930s.
(Photo courtesy of Ellis Kaiser).

the fishermen could take a break. Within a couple of hours they set out to retrieve it.

Shortly after they started hauling in the trawl, the sky became overcast and the wind began to increase. All of the crew were keeping a close eye on the weather, and as soon as William Munden and Levi Hardy had their trawl hauled back, they returned to the *Percy F. Russell* to off-load their catch, some 3,000 pounds of cod. Once the catch was off-loaded, the dory was taken aboard. The crew on board worked at putting away the fish and fishing gear as they waited for the second dory. As time passed, the weather conditions began to worsen due to a storm moving into the area.

Shortly before William Buffett and Percival Thomas had their trawl retrieved, a wave broke on deck of the *Percy F. Russell* and flooded the engine room. This caused the engine to stall and washed away the 3,000 pounds of fish that was on the deck.

Moments later, just when Percival and William were nearing the end of their trawl, another wave broke on the dory, and quickly filled it with water. Percival cut the trawl, hoping the dory would drift away, but another wave broke and capsized the craft, throwing the two men into the freezing water of the Atlantic. William Buffett surfaced close to the dory, but was unable to reach it. Percival Thomas surfaced alongside the dory and climbed up onto the bottom of it. He threw William Buffett a keg buoy, hoping he could grab onto it, so he could pull him back onto the dory. William Buffett couldn't reach the life-line and disappeared beneath the surface.

Samuel Thomas was standing in the rigging watching the incident unfold and shouted to the crew on deck. William Munden and Levi Hardy launched their dory at once, and with all their might, tried to row to Percival Thomas who was clinging to the bottom of the dory in freezing temperatures. Munden and Hardy finally reached the dory, but in the first attempt that William Munden tried to reach Percival, a wave broke and carried their dory some 100 feet away. With all their strength, William and Levi managed to row back to the overturned dory, and finally this time, they were able to pull Percival aboard. They then returned to the *Percy F. Russell*, but by which time, Percival was suffering exposure and barely conscious.

The *Percy F. Russell* arrived in North Sydney with her flag at half-mast to report the loss of William Buffett, along with another schooner, the *Yafico*, who was fishing nearby the *Percy F. Russell* and was missing three dories and six fishermen.

As for William Munden, this was not his first time saving a life. Just the previous spring on May 6, 1936, while lobster fishing in Garia Bay, just east of Petites, William saved the life of another fisherman, and was later award the Royal Canadian Humane Society Medal of Bravey.

Although William Munden and Levi Hardy had done what anyone would have, it was their hard work and bravery that saved the life of Percival Thomas.

Just two years after the incident, William Munden and Levi Hardy were both recognized for their effort and were presented with the Carnegie Medal. The medal was first established by Andrew Carnegie in the United States on April 15, 1904, and was presented to anyone who conducted an act of bravery.

Along with the bronze medal came a reward of $1,000. William Munden and Levi Hardy knew what they did was what many people would have done. They thus refused to accept the medal thinking they probably didn't deserve it, but surely they did as they had risked their lives, and for that reason, Percevial Thomas was spared his.

Eventually they accepted the reward and the money. William Munden invested his money back exactly were he earned it, on the sea. Shortly after receiving the money, he purchased a small skiff named the MV *Ethel J. Roy*.

William Munden and his crew became quite successful in the *Ethel J. Roy*, but again it didn't come easy. On October 22, 1940, Captain Munden and his crew of Nathan LeMoine, Fred Mauger, Eric Courtney, and William Hardy were fishing along the coast of Cape Breton near Glace Bay along with some of the other fishing fleet. Late that afternoon, the fishing grounds were battered by strong northeast winds.

Although the crew managed to get back on board, they were unable to get the dories aboard the skiff, and through the night, they were capsized by the winds and waves. Eventually, one broke loose and drifted away, but the other remained tied to the skiff.

Throughout the night of the storm, the *Ethel J. Roy* and her crew did everything they could to keep the skiff afloat and indeed it did work. Late the next evening, the *Ethel J. Roy* arrived back in Glace Bay. Two other skiffs, the MV *Carolina Moon* out of Diamond Cove, Newfoundland, under command of Captain Henry Spicer, and the MV *Eva Billard,* under command of Captain Gabriel Billard, out of Rose Blanche, were also caught in the same storm. Fortunately, Captain Billard was lucky enough to seek shelter at Port Morien and the *Carolina Moon* managed to seek shelter on the lee side of Scaterie Island. Because of this, they arrived in nearby Glace Bay the next day.

Others in the fleet were not so fortunate. One of the smaller skiffs caught in the storm was the MV *Alvin W* out of Glace Bay, under command of Captain Walter Pink. Along with Captain Pink, was his son Alvin and John Turner. Through the night, the *Alvin W* was beached on Scaterie Island and the crew were saved. Another skiff fishing that day which was not fortunate. The 48-foot MV *Bluebeard*, under command of Captain John Hayman from Fox Island, Newfoundland, and his crew of Ambrose Nash, Samuel Warren, Frank Hill, and John Garland all from Newfoundland, were never heard from again.

Although the storm was a harrowing experience for everyone, William Munden continued to fish the *Ethel J. Roy*, and several years later, he and his crew made the headlines again. In December of 1944, the *Ethel J. Roy* arrived in Glace Bay with 17,000 pounds of cod for one day's catch. The catch amount was valued at $680. A fine day's work in 1944 to say to the least.

By the late 1940s, the *Ethel J. Roy* had been battered by wind and waves for some twenty years. As a result, in 1947, William sold the sturdy little skiff to William Sheppard of North Sydney. After that he bought a 35-foot longliner named the MV *X10U8*, which he fished until 1958. After selling the *X10U8*, William Munden went to work

The crew of the *Ethel J. Roy* in December 1944. Front Row (l-r) Benjamin Vickers, Captain William Munden, and Alexander Anderson. Back Row: (l-r) George Brown, Levi Hardy, and Charles Purchase. (Author's Collection).

at the Naval Base in Point Edward, Nova Scotia, as a labourer. From there, he worked several odd jobs and finally went to work in construction, building high-rise apartment buildings. Unfortunately, while working on one of these sites in Sydney, he fell and injured his head and back. He passed away in 1983 at the age of eighty-one.

Captain George Thomas continued to command the *Percy F. Russell* for another two years. In the early hours of June 29, 1939,

The MV *X10U8* being launched in Glace Bay in May of 1948. Standing on the bow from (l-r) are George Brown, William Munden, Margruite Holtzhauer, Reg Munden, and Charles Purchase. (Photo courtesy of Reg Munden).

Captain Thomas and his crew departed North Sydney destined for the fishing grounds. Also outbound at the time was the MV *Domby*, a coal carrier en route to Montreal. At 06:00, both vessels collided while navigating in dense fog in the vicinity of Low Point. The bow of the *Domby* sliced the *Percy F. Russell* nearly in half, giving Captain Thomas and his crew barely enough time to launch a dory and row to safety. They lost everything they had aboard the skiff.

Captain Thomas still returned to the sea for several more years, and after he retired from the fishery, he went to work as a foreman in Leonard Brother's fish plant in North Sydney. In his later years, he returned to Harbour Le Cou, where he was born. He passed away there in 1962 at the age of eighty.

Samuel Thomas went to work in the Merchant Navy during the war, and then went to work on the Great Lakes. After several years on the lakes, Samuel went back to the fishery, fishing aboard trawers out of Louisbourg. On February 20, 1965, Samuel was a crew member aboard the side trawler MV *Cape Fortune*, and while fishing on the Grand Banks, he became ill and passed away. The trawler arrived in Halifax on February 22, 1965. His body was taken to

The shipwreck crew of the MV *Percy F. Russell* in 1939. Front row (l-r) George Best, Captain George Thomas, and James Hardy. Back row (l-r) unknown, unknown, and Albert Thorne. (Photo courtesy of Edith Moulton).

North Sydney and laid to rest. He was forty-seven years old at the time.

Percival Thomas later served in World War II, and then took part in commercial shipping, visiting ports all over the world. After his sailing career, he went to work as a stevedore at the ferry terminal in North Sydney. He passed away on February 2, 1966, at the age of fifty-six.

Levi Hardy also joined the Merchant Navy, and in 1942, he was serving aboard the SS *Lord Strathcona*, along with his son Gordon who was seventeen years old at the time. On September 5, 1942, the SS *Lord Strathcona* was torpedoed and sank in Conception Bay. Levi and his son Gordon survived, but Levi lost his medal of bravery he carried with him so proudly. Levi remained at sea for several more years, but then returned to the fishery in Ingonish. He passed away on February 3, 1974.

As for William Buffett, his body was never found. He was twenty-four years old when he was lost.

The Wreck of the Ruth Marie

The community of Burgeo, on the southwest coast of Newfoundland, was well-known in the days of schooner and foreign fish trade. The town was the location of the Moulton firm, one of the largest firms in the foreign trade on the south and southwest of the island. They often loaded fish in ports like Petites, Burgeo, and Ramea for the foreign market in places such as Spain, Portugal, West Indies, and South America.

The town of Burgeo was not only the home port for the large tern schooners, it was also the home of many master mariners who sailed them. Captain Maxwell Vatcher was one of them. Captain Vatcher was well-known in the shipping circle, and not only did he sail some of the largest tern schooners in the Moulton fleet, he also sailed smaller schooners around the coast of Newfoundland and Nova Scotia.

Like many sailors to cross the Atlantic in the days of sail, Captain Vatcher's career, while in command of the foreign-going ships, was far from uneventful. The first incident occured in the summer of 1920, while in command of the *Clarence A. Moulton.*

Captain Vatcher and his crew departed North Sydney, with a full cargo of coal for France, some 3,000 miles across the Atlantic. On August 28, 1920, while still in the middle of the ocean, a fire erupted on board the *Clarence A. Moulton.* The crew gave all their effort in trying to extinguish the fire, but they were unable to do so. As a result, they had no choice but to abandon the burning schooner.

Although they lost all of their belongings, they were fortunate enough to be picked up shortly after and were taken to Montreal by a passing ship.

Captain Vatcher returned home and then took command of another tern schooner for the Moulton firm named the *Ena A. Moulton.* For several years he commanded the *Ena A. Moulton,* until the early 1930s, when he decided to purchase a schooner of his own. With the schooner, he would carry supplies between Newfoundland and the mainland for merchants along the south and southwest coast.

In the fall of 1938, Captain Maxwell Vatcher purchased a schooner, the 57-foot *Ruth Marie,* which was built in Ireland's Eye, Trinity Bay, in 1935, by Plymouth Cooper. Since her launching, the *Ruth Marie* was used in the Labrador fishery and this would be her first in the coasting trade.

For the next several years, Vatcher and his crew had great success transporting goods on the *Ruth Marie.* In December 1942, he along with his two crew members, Cecil Buckland and William Billard, also from Burgeo, were making a routine voyage to North Sydney to pick up a load of cargo for the merchants back home.

With mid-December approaching, Captain Vatcher and his crew knew that this would probably be one of the last trips for the season.

MV *Ruth Marie* anchored in Ireland's Eye, Trinity Bay in 1935.
(Photo courtesy of Cooper Family).

In the late hours of December 10, 1942, the *Ruth Marie* had finished loading, and in the early hours of December 11, they departed North Sydney for the 130-mile journey home to Burgeo.

By late evening of December 11, the *Ruth Marie* was making its way east along the Newfoundland coast and passing the entrance to Connoire Bay, some fifteen miles west of Burgeo. By this time, the wind had begun to blow from the southeast and the sea began to build. As time progressed, the wind continued to increase and Captain Vatcher knew that sooner or later he would probably be experiencing poor visibility from a mixture of snow and rain, plus the fact that the sea was getting rougher. With these factors in mind, and along with the fact that the waters around Burgeo Islands are covered in treacherous shoals, Vatcher changed course and veered for shelter to the leeward. He eventually decided to anchor for the night in Grand Bruit Harbour, some thirteen miles to the west.

Within an hour, the *Ruth Marie* arrived in Grand Bruit Harbour and decided he would anchor in the northwest arm. As soon as he had the schooner turned around in the arm, he ordered the two anchors dropped. The anchors were let go with lots of chain to provide the schooner with a good holding ground throughout the night.

By midnight, the winds were blowing strong and the fishermen in Grand Bruit were all out checking their fishing boats and their moorings. George Billard, who was a teenager at the time, was standing on top of the hill with his parents. From were they were standing, they could see the *Ruth Marie* anchored in the harbour. George's father Henry was keeping a close watch on his 44-foot skiff, the *Melida J.*, that was moored further up in the harbour.

Although Captain Vatcher and his crew thought that the two anchors along with the long lead of chain would keep the *Ruth Marie* securely positioned throughout the night, they were wrong. Shortly after midnight, the anchors broke loose and the heavy laden *Ruth Marie* began to pound upon the rocks of Grand Bruit Harbour.

At this point, the destiny of the *Ruth Marie* and her cargo was sealed, so Captain Vatcher and his crew lowered a dory over the side to abandon the sinking schooner. Within no time, they reached the shoreline as they watched the schooner sink in the shallow water of northwest arm.

The local residents took Captain Vatcher and his crew into their homes and gave them food. Several days later, they found passage home to Burgeo on the coastal boat.

Although the *Ruth Marie* was only seven years old at the time, the pounding from the wind and seas was more than she could handle, and she was eventually beaten to pieces. Some of the local residents manage to salvage some of her cargo, but the majority of it rests on the bottom of the harbour.

Dorymen From the Freda M

The evolution of computers has had a tremendous effect on workers in every industry in today's world. For fishermen, computers improved the way of life in more ways than one, with weather reporting and projecting being very important.

Long before the days of weather equipment such as satellite radars, Ocean Data Acquisition Systems (ODAS), buoys, and computers, the availability of forecasting was limited. Apart from a forecast for the general area, the only other means that fishermen had to go by was a barometer and past experience. With not much to rely on, the fishermen were in times close in their predictions, and in many cases, dangers and disaster were averted. However, there were times when the weather conditions that evolved were far from their guesses, and in many cases, tragedy was inevitable.

In the winter of 1944, the southcoast fishing fleet of skiffs and schooners had again returned to the ports of Rose Blanche, Burnt Islands, and Port aux Basques to begin the winter fishery on the western shore. On the morning of February 12, 1944, the fleet went back to the banks to fish. The only forecast heard at the time predicted the weather to be east and southeast winds for the marine areas east of Sable Island.

Winds from this direction in the areas along the southwest coast, caused swells and seas to build, along with either snow or rain depending on the season and temperature. Although the weather forecast was not what some of the fishermen would call favourable, a portion of the fleet had returned to the fishing grounds again. A few of the vessels fishing on Rose Blanche Bank that mid-February morning were the MV *Eva Billard* (Captain Art Parsons), MV *Dulcie Anne* (Captain James Buffet), MV *Freda M* (Captain George Follett), and MV *Minnie & Muriel* (Captain Joseph Ashford). Fishing further to the east, in another well-known fishing ground named Burgeo Bank, were the MV *Rameaux* (Captain Rueben Carter) and MV *Margaret M. Riggs* (Captain George La Fosse).

The largest of the schooners fishing that day was the *Freda M*, a 116-foot; 12-dory banker built in Shelburne, Nova Scotia in 1928. She was owned jointly between Captain Follett and a firm in Grand Bank name G & A Buffett.

Captain George Follett was well-experienced and well-known in the bank fishery, mainly as a "high liner." On the morning of February 12, 1944, he knew that there was a possibility that a mixture of wet snow and rain may accompany the easterly and southeast winds. He also realized that if the wind was to gradually increase, then the sea would mostly likely build as well. With this in mind, Captain Follett informed his dorymen that if they should experience any such

MV *Freda M* in Halifax Harbour in 1961. (Holloway photo).

weather conditions, and fail to make the schooner, they were to remain by the keg of the trawl. Captain Follett knew he would find the keg in poor visibility, and hopefully he'd find the dorymen if the visibility decreased.

Shortly after the dories were launched, the wind began to increase from the east, and like many fishermen predicted, there also came snow. Earlier that morning, further down the coast, the winds had increased substantially. A eight-dory banker named the *Beatrice Grace*, under command of Captain George Newport, had departed Hare Harbour, Fortune Bay, earlier that morning after taking on herring for bait. Shortly after his departure, the schooner encountered easterly wind and snow, so Captain Newport decided to seek shelter in the port of Fortune.

On Burgeo Bank, the wind and snow was playing devil's advocate, which in turn resulted in disaster. The easterly wind brought snow with near zero visibility shortly after Captain Rueben Carter of the *Rameaux* had lowered his eight dories and sixteen men. In no time, he had realized that his dories and dorymen had gone astray. Fortunately between the *Rameaux* and the *Margaret M. Riggs* seven of the dories and fourteen of its crew were later picked up. The eighth dory carrying John Robert Porter and his son Harvey were not so fortunate. They were nowhere to be found. The schooners continued to search the fishing grounds, but the dory nor the father-son team were seen again. John Robert was thirty-seven and his son Harvey was seventeen.

Further to the westward, the fishermen on Rose Blanche Bank were also doing everything in their effort to get back to port. Captain Art Parsons in the two-dory banker *Eva Billard*, had made landfall at Bras Hills, just to the west of Rose Blanche. Fortunately, they arrived back in their home port safely.

Captain Follett was in the process of retrieving his twelve dories as well. Unfortunately, trying to get twelve aboard with its crew and contents takes considerable time. Hence, for some of the crew, there was not enough time. Out of the twelve dories lowered away that February morning, only ten returned.

After searching a short while, Captain Follett came upon the kegs belonging to the two dories, but the dory and occupants were nowhere to be seen.

There was no doubt that the fishermen had taken the word of Captain Follett and did indeed stay on the keg. Whether the dories were swamped from being held down by the trawl, or if the fishermen cut the trawl and had simply driven out to sea in the hope of being saved, no one knows.

After retrieving the kegs, Captain Follett searched the remainder of the day and throughout the night. However, at daylight the next morning, there was still no sign of the strayed crewmen. In such strong winds and high seas, the fishermen could not have survived.

After searching the area, Captain Follett returned to Rose Blanche to report the lost of the crew members to G & A Buffet at Grand Bank, who then reported the loss to the families. The crew lost from the *Freda M* that disastrous day were:

> Alan Price
> Bert Price
> Wilson Green
> Archibald Scott

As for Captain Follett, he continued to command the *Freda M* for the next seventeen years, and in the later years, he turned to the coasting trade. The *Freda M* first escaped disaster in February 1948, while secured to the dock in Fortune. The ice in the river broke clear and carried a number of vessels out of the harbour and aground. Fortunately, the *Freda M* suffered only minor damage.

However, in the fall of 1961, the end would come to the well-known lady of the Atlantic. On the night of October 7, 1961, the *Freda M* was en route to Newfoundland with a load of coal. Shortly after Captain Follett retired to his cabin for the night, he heard the sound of cracking wood. When he ran to the deck, he discovered that his vessel had collided with a freighter named the MV *Merchant*

Royal. The *Freda M* sank immediately. Captain Follett's and his crew were lucky and escaped the sinking vessel.

Not far from the distressed ship was another well-known schooner named the MV *Nina W. Corkum* under the command of Captain Banfield.

Fortunately for the crew, they all survived, but the *Freda M's* career had come to an end after thirty-three years. Captain George Follett returned to the sea in the MV *Nellie Cluett*, and several years later, he retired. He passed away in 1973 at the age of eighty.

Crew member Wilson Green. (Photo courtesy of Wilson Green).

The Adventures of Captain Thomas Chislett

The community of Rose Blanche, has become well-known throughout the years with respect to the fishery, as well as some of the fishermen who were from there. One such man was Thomas "Tom" Chislett.

Tom Chislett was born in Rose Blanche in 1912, and began his career dory fishing at the age of thirteen under a fisherman named Jacob Hatcher. After several years, Tom went shareman with another local fisherman named Arthur Moore, where he fished aboard two small skiffs named the MV *Active* and *Bonny B*. Tom fished several years with Arthur Moore and later married his daughter. Tom and his wife settled down in Rose Blanche and had three children.

But they did not settle for long. In 1947, many fishermen from the southwest coast were relocating to the booming ports of Nova Scotia and Tom decided to do the same. As a result, he and his wife, along with their three children, relocated to Glace Bay, Nova Scotia. Once there, Tom went to work as a labourer in a fish plant that was owned and operated by P. J. Cadegan Ltd.

Although he enjoyed the work in the fish plant, Tom's love for going to sea and fishing was still in his blood. Thus, he decided to return to the fishing industry. For his first few years back in the fishery, he commanded several small longliners out of Glace Bay, such as the MV *Miss Cape Breton* and the MV *Jessie Louise*.

In the winter of 1951, Tom joined the crew of the MV *Phyllis &*

James, a 53-foot skiff out of Glace Bay, under command of Captain Charles Munden. Then in the spring of 1951, Tom took command of the *Phyllis & James*, when Captain Munden went to work in the lobster fishery.

In the fall of 1951, Captain Chislett took command of the MV *Sara Morton*, a 62-foot fish carrier owned by P. J. Cadegan Ltd. The Cadegan firm also bought fish in Rose Blanche. Captain Chislett would load the fish at Rose Blanche and unload the fish at the Cadegan processing plant in Glace Bay.

By the early 1950s, a new era evolved in the fishing industry when the new design of longliners came onto the scene. The longliners became very popular, and fishermen from all over were placing orders to have them built. One firm in North Sydney, Leonard Brothers Ltd.,

The MV *Lenarfish* outbound Mahone Bay on her maiden voyage in June 1956. (Photo courtesy of Wesley Kendall).

had ordered several of the new longliners built as well. Captain Chislett was offered to take command of the first vessel to be launched, so in 1955, Chislett retired his command of the *Sara Morton*.

Before taking command of the new longliner, Captain Chislett relocated his family from Glace Bay to North Sydney. Then in June of 1956, Chislett and his crew arrived in Mahone Bay, Nova Scotia, to take command of the new longliner; the 57-foot MV *Lenarfish* which had just been launched from the Maclean's Shipyard.

After the sea trials were carried out, and everything was found in good working order, the *Lenarfish* departed Mahone Bay, on her maiden voyage. Her destination was the swordfishing grounds off Sable Island.

From the very first trip, Captain Chislett and his crew became very successful in the new longliner, and as the year progressed, the rewards continued. As a result, the very next year, Captain Chislett decided to have his own longliner built.

By this time however, the shipyards around Nova Scotia were busy filling previous orders, and it seemed that the captain was out of luck. Still however, Captain Chislett kept trying, and finally his luck changed

MV *Anne Denise* outbound Chester, Nova Scotia, on her maiden voyage in September 1957. (Photo courtesy of Emery Stevens).

when he met the owners of a shipyard in Chester, Nova Scotia, named Chester Seacraft Industries. Although the shipyard normally built smaller boats, the owners decided to look at the plans. Consequently, they were reviewed by a Dutch naval architect named Thomas Timmerman, who was working at the shipyard at the time. Mr. Timmerman had designed a model as Captain Chislett preferred and then went ahead with the construction. Then in the fall of 1957, the MV *Anne Denise*, named after the captain's daughter, was launched.

The *Anne Denise* had a length of fifty-seven feet and a width of seventeen and was powered with a 190 HP Rolls Royce. After the launching and the sea trials were carried out, the *Anne Denise* departed Chester for her home port of North Sydney. At North Sydney, the trawl and fishing supplies were loaded. By now it was too late for swordfishing, so the *Anne Denise* departed North Sydney on a cod fishing trip around Anticosti Island in the Gulf of St. Lawrence. The crew consisted of:

> Thomas Chislett, North Sydney
> Nathan LeMoine, Rose Blanche
> Eli Chislett, Rose Blanche
> Montford Chislett, Rose Blanche
> Samuel Brown, Rose Blanche
> George Leonard Jr. Supernumery, North Sydney

Captain Chislett's success aboard the *Anne Denise* continued just like the days on the *Lenarfish*, but unfortunately the career of the the new vessel was short lived.

In the summer of 1963, Captain Chislett decided not to participate in the swordfishery, and instead, he went fishing for halibut in the Gulf of St. Lawrence, starting around Antcosti Island and making his way along the lower north shore of Quebec.

By mid-September, Captain Chislett and his crew were making their way back to Rose Blanche. There some of the crew could disembark to be with their families. From there, Chislett and the remaining crew would return home to North Sydney, so they could spend time with their families as well.

In early evening of September 21, 1963, the *Anne Denise* departed Bonne Bay, on the west coast of Newfoundland, for the 100-mile journey to Rose Blanche. The crew consisted of:

> Thomas Chislett, captain, North Sydney
> Montford Chislett, deckhand, Rose Blanche
> Thomas Hatcher, deckhand, Rose Blanche
> Cecil Hardy, deckhand, Rose Blanche
> Edward Riles, cook, West Point
> Gilbert Riles, deckhand, West Point

The beginning of the voyage went well, and early the next morning, the *Anne Denise* was passing the entrance of St. George's Bay. At 06:00, crew member Thomas Hatcher was alone in the wheelhouse conducting his watch, as the remaining crew were resting down below. A little while later, Thomas discovered smoke down in the engineroom and alerted Captain Chislett at once.

Immediately, Chislett and the rest of the men hurried to the wheelhouse to investigate the smoke and discovered the engineroom was one big blaze and already burning out of control. The *Anne Denise*, like all longliners, had the fuel tanks for the main engine in the engineroom. Captain Chislett feared that the fire would cause the fuel tanks to explode so he ordered the crew to ready the dory.

As the crew launched the small craft, the fire raged on. Captain Chislett immediately told his crew to abandon the burning longliner at once. Now they had to row to the nearest land mass which was the community of Codroy, Newfoundland, some twenty-two miles away.

At 20:00, after rowing for over twelve hours, the tired crew members beached their dory at Codroy. Some of the residents, who saw the dory far off on the horizon with six men on board became curious, but once they discovered what had happened, they directed them to the local boarding house of John Dalton, where they spent the night. The next morning, a truck belonging to the fish merchant at Port aux Basques picked them up and carried them back.

Although the experience could have been a more disastrous one, it didn't keep the crew from fishing. For two of the crew members, Edward Riles and his son Gilbert, this had been the second time in four years where they had to abandon their vessel due to fire.

Shortly after the loss of the *Anne Denise*, Captain Chislett took command of another longliner for Leonard Brothers Ltd. named MV *George III*. Once here for a short time, he was then given the opportunity to take command of another longliner named the MV *Dorthea Reeves*, which was also owned by Leonard Brothers Ltd. The 63-foot *Dorthea Reeves* had been built in Fortune, in 1959, by R. & L. Grandy Ltd. Her previous captain was George Kendall from North Sydney, formerly of Ramea.

Captain Chislett continued to fish for halibut, cod, and swordfish in the *Dorothea Reeves*, just as he did in his previous commands. In the latter part of March 1969, the *Dorothea Reeves* and her seven man crew departed North Sydney for a routine halibut trip. The fishing grounds were in the vicinity of St. Paul's Island, off the north tip of Cape Breton.

After several days fishing, Captain Chislett and his crew began to experience bad weather. The captain then decided that after the weather improved, he would try fishing closer to Newfoundland. Hence, he decided to stopover at Rose Blanche so some of the crew could spend some time with their families.

On Saturday, March 29, 1969, the *Dorothea Reeves* arrived in Rose Blanche. Once there, crew members Ronald Parsons, Alexander Spicer, Gerald Best, and Clayton Lillington went to their respective homes.

Early Sunday morning, the *Dorothea Reeves* departed Rose Blanche for the nearby community of West Point so crew member Edward Riles would be able to spend time with his family as well. Making the trip with Captain Chislett and Edward Riles was crew member Garland Hayman who, like Captain Chislett, was now residing in North Sydney.

Shortly after breakfast, the *Dorothea Reeves* arrived at the new government dock in West Point. Captain Chislett and Garland Hayman joined Edward Riles at his home in nearby Stone's Harbour, just less than a mile's walk from were the vessel was berthed.

Shortly after lunch, Chislett decided he would be returning to Burgeo Bank to fish once he had all the crew picked up. As Chislett was making his way from the home of Edward Riles to the dock where the *Dorthea Reeves* was secured, he was met by a local fisherman, who informed him that there was smoke coming from the vessel.

Captain Chislett and his crew hurried to the dock at once, and when they arrived, they discovered smoke billowing from the engine-room of the longliner. The fire would be difficult to fight with the smoke and heat. The blaze also posed a possible threat to nearby houses, whaves, and fishing stages. All could easily ignite if the burning hull was not taken away from the dock and out of the harbour immediately.

The ropes of the longliner were cut instantly and two fishermen from the community, Hubert Riles and Chesley Vautier, boarded their 35-foot longliner, the MV *Arlene Bernette*, and secured a towline to the *Dorothea Reeves* in the hope of towing her out of the harbour. The fishermen were successful, and when she posed no further threat, the towline was cut. The fire raged as the longliner drifted near a beach just west of the harbour. The underwater portion sank in the shallow water near Poile Point.

The crew of the *Dorothea Reeves* lost everything, even their catch of halibut, which was approximately 7,000 pounds, plus several thousands pounds of cod. The crew returned home and the loss of the longliner was reported to the owners.

Captain Chislett was not without a vessel very long, but the *Dorothea Reeves* was the last vessel he commanded for Leonard Brothers Ltd. His next command was the 58-foot MV *Nancy N*, which was owned by H. B. Nickerson & Sons Ltd. of North Sydney.

Chislett fished the *Nancy N* until 1971, when he took command of the 91-foot longliner MV *Vair*, which was also owned by the same company. However, by the early 1970s, the swordfishery was declining, and crew for the large longliners were becoming more difficult to find. With these factors in hand, Captain Chislett gave up commanding longliners and took command of a 59-foot fish carrier named the MV *Alma Griffin*.

Captain Chislett ran the *Alma Griffin* from 1974 until the early 1980s, carrying salmon from Labrador ports to Sandy Cove, on the Northern Peninsula. From Sandy Cove, the salmon were trucked to Port aux Basques, then carried to the Nickerson fish plant in North Sydney by the gulf ferries.

MV *Alma Griffin* at Port Greville in 1958. (Photo courtesy of the Wagstaff Collection, Age of Sail Heritage Centre, Port Greville NS).

Carrying salmon on the Labrador normally ran from late spring until late fall. After the Labrador, Chislett took the *Alma Griffin* along the coast of Nova Scotia, picking up herring from the seiners, and taking it to the plant in Canso, Nova Scotia.

By the mid-1980s, these fisheries were declining and Captain Chislett gave up going to sea all together. He then went to work as a security watchman at a fish plant in North Sydney. However, shortly after retiring, he did go to sea one more time. In the fall of 1983, Chislett took command of the 65-foot longliner, MV *Sandra Carolann* for several trips while her regular captain, Richard "Dick" Hardy returned home to attend a funeral.

MV *Sandra Carolann* tied at the T. J. Hardy's fish plant in Port aux Basques in 1983. (Author's Collection).

This would be Captain Chislett's last trip at sea. He later developed Alzheimer's and passed away at North Sydney in 1992 at the age of eighty.

Tom Chislett in 1983. (Photo courtesy of Dennis Chislett).

The Life and Times of the Chislett Brothers

Some of the most common incidents and misfortunes that happen at sea involved collisions, groundings, sinkings, explosions, and fires. Any seaman or fisherman who has been unfortunate enough to be involved in such an incident often says that one of the worst situations to experience at sea is a fire or an explosion.

Depending of course on the circumstances, an explosion is probably one of the worst things that can happen at sea. First of all, in most cases, they occur without warning, giving the crew little or no time to save themselves. Second, escape routes and exits sometimes become blocked. The final result is that crew and passengers are left trapped inside to burn to death. Last of all, in many cases, lifesaving equipment becomes damaged or destroyed, sometimes in the best of weather, leaving a distressed sailor to retreat to the open ocean. This being the case, survival is often slim.

The community of Rose Blanche has been the home to many fishermen over the years, and a port often visited by fishermen from other areas as well. John Chislett was born and raised in Rose Blanche and went fishing at an early age. He and his wife raised three sons and one daughter. John, like many fishermen, had a 45-foot skiff named the MV *Brenda Chislett,* and as soon as his sons were old enough to go, they joined him.

In the spring of 1944, sixty-two-year-old John Chislett and this three sons: Walter aged twenty-eight, Eli aged twenty-six, and George aged twenty-four, were preparing for a routine spring fishing trip on board the

Brenda Chislett. On Thursday morning, May 25, 1944, the *Brenda Chislett* departed Rose Blanche for the spring and summer fishery along the coast of Cape Breton. Their destination for this trip was St. Paul's Island, some sixty miles away, off the north tip of Cape Breton Island. The voyage to the fishing grounds went well, and the *Brenda Chislett* anchored at the end of the island near Goat Rock early that evening.

Shortly after they were anchored, the fishermen were preparing for the next day's fishing. One of the main priorities was to refill the vessel's engine with gas. This was the normal practice and had been done many times before. As the engine was being filled, the crew was unaware that some of the gasoline fumes had drifted forward and all throughout the hull of the skiff.

Moments after the engine's tanks were filled, and the crew was finishing up their chores, an explosion erupted aboard the *Brenda Chislett.* The shock blew the main deck off completely, along with the dory and water barrel.

Although the blast had totally destroyed the skiff, the crew managed to survive. George had fallen down into the hold of the skiff that burst into flames immediately after the explosion. Walter, who was the only crew member down below at the time of explosion, made his way forward where the deck was blown off. Eli and his father were thrown into the air and overboard.

Although John and his sons had survived the blast, two of them did not escape without injury. George suffered burns to his face and hands, but still managed to abandon the burning skiff by jumping over the side. Walter suffered severe burns to his hands and also on his face, with the worst being near his eyes. He decided to remain on board the skiff near the bow.

Anchored not far from the *Brenda Chislett* was another skiff from Rose Blanche named the MV *Nora Harriett.* Its captain, Jacob Hatcher, immediately set course for the distressed fishermen.

First they picked up John, who could not swim, then George and Eli. They then returned to the burned hull of the *Brenda Chislett* to pick up Walter.

Captain Hatcher and his crew offered the best first aid they could and departed the area for the closest port which was White Point. From there, Captain Hatcher took them to Neil's Harbour where they were treated by Dr. MacDonald, who gave the fishermen the best treatment he had available. He then advised the fishermen that it would be in their best interest if they went to the hospital in North Sydney for further treatment.

Captain Hatcher and his crew carried out the doctor's orders, and departed Neil's Harbour at once, arriving in North Sydney on the afternoon of May 26. There, the four fishermen, were admitted to the hospital for further care.

Several days later, the four fishermen were discharged and returned home to their families. Although the mishap could have easily been fatal, it did not keep John Chislett and his sons away from the fishery.

It would not be long before the family wanted a replacement for the *Brenda Chislett*, but all of the local shipyards were filled with orders, and they would be unable to get a new vessel for two years. The men need-ed to fish and needed a boat, so while they were waiting for their new skiff to be built, they bought an older boat in Rose Blanche, the 38-foot MV *Primrose*, which they renamed the MV *W T Chislett*. Now John and his three sons were ready to go back fishing.

They fished the *W T Chislett* until the summer of 1946, when they took delivery of their new skiff, the 47-foot MV *H B Chislett*, which was launched from the shipyard of Edward Farrell at North Bay, La Poile late that spring. By now, John was nearing retirement age, so Walter became sole owner and commanded the *H B Chislett*. Walter's two brothers made up the crew as well as several other fish-ermen from Rose Blanche. During the summer months, they often went swordfishing along the coast of Nova Scotia.

However, during the 1950s, the new design of longliners was being introduced to the fishery. As a result, Eli left his two brothers in 1956, to join his cousin, Captain Tom Chislett, who had just taken command of a new longliner named the MV *Lenarfish*.

Walter and the remainder of the crew fished the *H B Chislett* for several more years, but unfortunately, it would not be long before she would meet her demise as well.

Early one May morning, Walter and George were en route to Garia Bay, just east of Rose Blanche, when a fire erupted in the engine-room. With only two of them on board, it was not long before the fire raged out of control, forcing them to abandon the burning skiff.

Now Walter and his crew were without a boat again, but not for long. Walter then went to Glace Bay and took command of a 52-foot longliner named the MV *Margaret Rose III*. While he and his crew were fishing the new vessel, he placed an order to have a boat built at the shipyard of R & L Grandy in Marystown. In the winter of 1964, the 45-foot MV *E.V.W.* (named after his wife Edna and daughter's Walterine and Valerie) was launched.

The three brothers reunited again to fish the new longliner, however only for a short time. The next year, George and his son Austin went fishing themselves in a small motorboat. Walter and Eli remained together aboard the *E.V.W.*

On the morning of November 26, 1969, Walter and his crew of Eli Chislett, Hubert Hatcher, James Hatcher, William Stroud, and Wesley Hatcher, all from Rose Blanche, awoke for another day of fishing. Early that morning, before anyone boarded the *E.V.W.*, a fire erupted in the

engineroom. When Walter arrived down on the dock, the fire was raging out of control. Walter and Hubert boarded a small row boat at once, and with all their might, managed to tow the burning long-liner out of the harbour near Bell Rock, fearing that nearby houses and wharves would be damaged or destroyed. The fire raged out of control until the *E.V.W.* was totally destroyed. Her remains sank three miles from Rose Blanche Harbour.

Eli Chislett at his home in Rose Blanche in 1979. (Photo courtesy of Dan Chislett).

Although the *E.V.W.* was the third fire Walter Chislett had experienced, it did not keep him from fishing. Shortly after the loss of the *E.V.W.*, he bought a small fishing boat and also ran a small general store. He later sold the boat and just worked the store. He passed away on April 13, 1981, at the age of sixty-five.

Eli remained to the end and spent several years fishing aboard the longliner MV *Debbie & Clara* with George Hayman of Rose Blanche. He later went to work as a lighthouse keeper on Caines Island, but retired after he suffered a heart attack. Eli, like his brother Walter, did not enjoy much of the retirement years. He passed away on April 26, 1983, at the age of sixty-five.

George on the other hand, remained in the fishery until he retired. After a short while fishing in their small motorboat, they bought the MV *Sarah B* from John Farrell in West Point. Several years later, they purchased a 33-foot longliner from Nova Scotia named the MV *Katrina* which was renamed the MV *Tracy Deanne*. In 1978, they took delivery of a new longliner, the 35-foot *Randy Deanne*, named after Austin's two children He passed way in November 2004, at the age of eighty.

George and Esther Chislett at Rose Blanche in the 1970s.
(Photo courtesy of Dan Chislett).

Crewman Lost From the
Mary J. W. Calman

During the early 1940s, the demand for fresh fish began to increase, and the result was an upswing in the fishery. All of the local shipyards around Newfoundland were busy launching boat after boat, many of them much bigger than the ones they had built before.

Also, along the south and southwest coast, was the construction of processing plants; a small one at La Poile, although it only lasted for several years, and a much larger one at Isle aux Morts. The processing plant at Isle aux Morts was one of the largest on the coast and required plenty of labourers. Men came from all along the south and southwest coast to help build the plant, and after it was built, they went to work processing fish.

One young man who came to work at the fish plant in Isle aux Morts was Walter Pink from Cape La Hune. He arrived with his wife and children in the hope of finding a brighter future. Who would know that their future would be marred by tragedy.

Just a couple years after relocating to the area, one of their sons Roy, was eager to join the workforce and thus signed aboard a schooner from Isle aux Morts named the MV *Mary J.W. Calman*. She was a 53-foot schooner owned and commanded by a well-known local fisherman named James Baggs.

In the fall of 1946, Captain Baggs was preparing the *Mary J.W. Calman* for the annual 'Fall Fishing,' a tradition where Newfoundland boats and men fished the waters off Cape Breton Island from October to late December.

The MV *Mary J.W. Calman* moored in Isle aux Morts in July 1959.
(Photo courtesy of Ruby Munden).

For Roy Pink, he could hardly wait, and for any young fisherman wanting to learn the techniques of the hook and line fishery, the *Mary J.W. Calman* would be just the place to learn.

On Monday October 7, 1946, the *Mary J.W. Calman* departed Isle aux Morts for the 100-mile voyage to North Sydney. The crew consisted of:

> James Baggs
> John Baggs
> George Seymour
> Philip Seymour
> Elias Lawrence
> Roy Pink

The beginning of the voyage was uneventful, but as the night drew on, the weather began to worsen, so that by early the next morning, the northerly wind was blowing at gale force with the sea gradually building. Around breakfast time the next morning, when the *Mary J.W. Calman* was still thirty miles out from the port of North Sydney, a huge wave crashed on the deck of the vessel, carrying away barrels of gasoline and everything that was moveable on deck. Unfortunately, Roy Pink was also standing on the deck at the time. He too was carried over the side.

The remainder of the crew hurried to the deck at once in the hope of catching a glimpse of the young fisherman. Tragically, Roy Pink was never seen again. With gale-force winds and rough seas, there was little the crew could do but to try and keep the schooner seaworthy and hope to reach the port of North Sydney. Finally, shortly after lunch, the *Mary J.W. Calman* arrived in North Sydney, some sixteen hours after leaving her home port.

Once there, Captain James Baggs would have to report the tragedy to the parents of the lost seaman. As the captain of the *Mary J.W. Calman*, he wanted to do it properly, so he returned home to Isle aux Morts by the CNR ferry to inform the Pink family of what had happened.

Obviously, the family was devastated with the loss of their son. After James Baggs had done his duty, he returned to Cape Breton to carry out the remainder of the fishing season. He continued to fish the *Mary J.W. Calman* until the late 1950s, when she was sold to foreign interests.

As for Walter and Berthina Pink, the loss of their son Roy would not be the end of their tragedy. On November 17, 1949, they were faced with another accident when their son Walter Jr. drowned while bird hunting near Rose Blanche along with a companion. Like his brother Roy, his body was never found.

Astray From the Margaret M. Riggs

During the days of the bank fishery, fishermen dealt with some sort of fear and danger everyday they fished. One of the most common threats was the fear of dories going astray. This thought was always on the minds of those who boarded the dories, but also to the captains.

The dories became separated for one simple reason, poor visibility, due to the sudden onset of snow or fog. Without being able to see the schooner, many dories lost their bearings and went astray.

In some instances, the dories and their occupants lived to tell of their experiences, such as being at sea for weeks with little or no food and water, and being picked up by other ships who carried them to distant ports. Some have even rowed hundreds of miles to land. Yet, most of these incidents had tragic outcomes where the dories or the fishermen were never heard from again.

Probably one of the most miraculous stories involving dories going astray was that of the banking schooner *Autauga*, a twelve-dory banker under the command of Captain Joseph Rose of Jersey Harbour, Newfoundland. One brisk morning in March 1936, Captain Rose and his crew were fishing on Burgeo Bank, off the southwest coast of Newfoundland. The weather consisted of a light southwest wind, so Captain Rose lowered his twelve dories and the fishermen rowed away to set their trawl. After the trawl was out, the fishermen returned to the schooner for a short break and quick lunch.

While on board the schooner, the wind veered from southwest to northwest and then to northeast. Captain Rose watched the change cautiously and decided that if the wind increased, he would not be sending his men back out. When the wind did not pick up, and the barometer gave no indications of a drop in pressure, Captain Rose ordered the crew to underrun their trawl.

Shortly after they started, the wind did increase, and a slight sea began to build. The temperature dropped below freezing and the visibility decreased to near zero from heavy snow squalls. As a result, all twelve dories lost sight of the schooner immediately. All night the twenty-four dorymen tossed about in the hungry seas. Early the next morning, when the snow lightened and the wind slackened, the schooner saw the twelve dories upon the horizon. A short while later, they were all taken aboard the *Autauga*; a close call to say the least.

Twelve years later, in 1948, another similar incident occurred involving the crew of the MV *Margaret M. Riggs*. The *Margaret M. Riggs* was a 72-foot, eight-dory banker built in Flat Island, Placentia Bay, in 1935, and owned by the Penny firm in Ramea.

In the spring of 1948, the *Margaret M. Riggs* departed her home port of Ramea for the fishing grounds of St. Pierre Bank, off the south coast of Newfoundland. Her crew consisted of the following:

George La Fosse, captain	James Well Young, doryman
Albert Kendall, engineer	William "Bill" Young, doryman
Wilbert Bowles, doryman	Harold Keeping, doryman
Eric Bowles, doryman	George Rossitier, doryman
John Thomas Bowles, doryman	George Robert Durnford, doryman
George Warren, doryman	Stan Pink, doryman
Nathan Warren, doryman	Ernest Barter, doryman
Norman MacDonald, doryman	Samuel Fudge, dorymen
Alexander MacDonald, doryman	Ben Crewe, dorymen

In June 1948, the *Margaret M. Riggs* was fishing on the northwest part of St. Pierre Bank, some 45-miles from her home port of Ramea.

On this beautiful June morning, the crew boarded the eight dories and rowed away to set out their trawl. Once set, the dories and their crews returned to the schooner for a brief stopover, then again boarded the dories to retrieve their trawl.

Shortly after they began to retrieve their trawl, a heavy bank of fog covered the fishing grounds, something not uncommon for this area, especially this time of year. Unfortunately, only four of the dories were able to make it back to the schooner. The remaining four dories had gone astray.

The MV *Margaret M. Riggs* at Halifax in the 1940s during refit.
(Photo courtesy of Hartley La Fosse).

Fortunately however, there was still some good luck in their favour. Later that evening, three of the four dories that went astray were able to make it back to the schooner. However, the fourth dory, which was occupied by Frank Bowles and George Warren was nowhere to be seen.

George Warren and Frank Bowles had not only experienced trouble with weather, they also experienced trouble with their trawl when it broke after becoming tangled in something on the seabed. The two dorymen then had to return to the keg on the opposite end in the hope of retrieving the remainder of the trawl.

By the time they reached the keg on the opposite end, the day was quickly passing by, and it was then that the fishing grounds became blanketed with fog. Now George Warren and Frank Bowles had more to worry about than the trawl, for they had to worry about making it back to the schooner. They knew their lives were in jeopardy.

Later that evening, while still enveloped in thick fog, darkness fell on the fishing grounds, and the two fishermen prepared themselves for the night.

Back on board the schooner, Captain La Fosse and his crew searched aimlessly for the dory and for their two shipmates. All the seamen knew, that with such poor visibility, chances of finding them were very slim.

Early the next morning, George Warren and Frank Bowles had thought their destiny changed for the better when the visibility increased and they could see a large white merchant ship on the horizon. This of course changed when the ship sailed by the two fishermen without seeing them.

Although they were not spotted the first time, later that day their luck did change when they sighted another vessel on the horizon. This time the vessel was much smaller and moving slowly.

Fortunately this time, the two fishermen would be in luck. The second vessel was the trawler MV *Mustang* out of Burin, under the command of Captain James Chaulk.

Finally at noon, the two fishermen and their dory were taken aboard the *Mustang*. Besides being a little hungry and tired, the two fishermen were in good condition. Captain Chaulk, however, could not report picking up the seaman immediately because his ship-to-shore radio was out of commission.

Early the next day, the *Mustang* finished fishing for the trip, and Captain Chaulk departed the fishing grounds for her home port of Burin. Although George Warren and Frank Bowles only spent one day astray from their schooner, it could have been much longer, and the end result could have been much different.

Frank Bowles remained in the fishery and passed away in his hometown of Ramea years later. George Warren however left the fishery several years later and resettled in Corner Brook, where he went to work in the paper mill until he retired.

As for the *Margaret M. Riggs*, she remained under the Penny management for several more years and was later sold to a local captain in Harbour Breton. On September 30, 1954, while en route to a south coast port from North Sydney, she sprang a leak and sank while loaded with coal.

Lost From the Betty & Audrey

The winter of 1949 saw the beginning of another winter fishery on the southwest coast of Newfoundland. The usual fleet of skiffs and schooners from along the coast had returned for another year of prosperous fishing.

As the winter progressed, the fishermen were being faced with another obstacle, besides the normal everyday obstacles of high winds, poor visibility, and rough seas. They were now beginning to find it difficult to secure bait for their trawls.

The problem was not only being experienced by the fishermen on the southwest coast, it was the same all along the coast. To assist with the problem, the government tried to help by helping them search for bait. Many places like Port aux Basques saw large numbers of schooners berthed at the wharf.

However things began to improve by mid-March, and some of the boats were beginning to pickup small amounts of bait in various places along the coast. One of the schooners fortunate enough to secure some bait, for at least one trip to the fishing grounds, was the MV *Betty & Audrey*, a 67-foot four-dory schooner under the command of a well-known captain named William "Bill" Banfield from Bay L'Argent, Fortune Bay.

Being unable to find enough bait was nothing new to Captain Banfield. With thirty-five years of sea time under his belt, he was no stranger to any difficult situation faced by bank fishermen. During his career, he commanded large 12-dory bankers such as the *Paloma* and the *James & Stanley*. Also during the war years, Captain Banfield served on oil tankers.

Although Banfield was lucky enough to secure some bait, he was still faced with another problem he had experienced before, not having a full crew. The *Betty & Audrey* normally carried four dories, but he only had enough for three, so he went on the hunt for two more.

To overcome this obstacle, Banfield returned to Port aux Basques where many vessels in the fleet lay tied up with no bait and idle crew members. At Port aux Basques he met another well-known captain named Edward Andrews, who was in command of MV *Man Alone*.

After a short conversation with Captain Andrews, mainly concerning the bait shortage, Captain Banfield discovered that Captain Andrews and his crew were also awaiting bait. With this in mind, Captain Banfield asked Captain Andrews if any of his crew would be interested in making a short trip in the meantime. Two of the crew members from the *Man Alone*, George Dollimount and his dorymate, were willing to make the trip and thus joined the *Betty & Audrey*. Finally on March 15, 1949, the *Betty & Audrey* departed Port aux Basques for the fishing grounds in the vicinity of Cape Anguille several miles away.

On Wednesday, March 16, the wind began to increase from the southeast and the sea began to build. By noon, the winds had changed to south-southwest and continued to intensify until reaching storm force.

The storm ravaged the area, and was later noted as being one of the worst to hit the area since 1918. The storm had caused the tide to rise higher than normal, and several fishing vessels sank at their moorings. A large barge owned by Bowater Paper Mill, which was secured at Port aux Basques, were it was used to store paper awaiting shipment, was torn away from its mooring and driven ashore on the rocks, later to be refloated.

The storm was not exactly unexpected to many of the local mariners. The date March 21, is the annual spring equinox, when day and night are equal, as the sun crosses the equator, making its way south. Local mariners refer to the equator as the 'line,' and every year, several days before the sun crosses this so called line, the area is normally hit by a storm known locally as a Line Breeze.

Captain Banfield knew about Line Breezes and also knew they

could be quite intense. Thus, with this in mind, he decided to return to port, but before doing so, he offered help to another schooner fishing in the area named the MV *Mack Mariner II.*

The *Mack Mariner II* was a three-dory schooner out of Port aux Basques under the command of Kenneth Currie of Rose Blanche. The storm that swept the fishing grounds had carried away nearly all of the vessel's canvas. Although the schooner was powered by an engine, it was of no use because the dry-cell batteries used to start the engine, had no charge.

Captain Banfield and his crew assisted the *Mack Mariner II* by securing a towline to the stricken vessel with the hope of getting her back to port safety. However, fate had another plan. The towline broke and both crews were unable to secure it again.

Now Captain Kenneth Currie and the crew of the *Mack Mariner II* were left to reach port on their own. The crew of the distressed schooner, besides the captain, had been picked up from ports all around the south coast such Cape La Hune, Cul de Sul, and Fox Island. They consisted of John Hardy, Walter Baggs, Samuel Baggs, Matthew Pink, George Pink, John Dollimount, and Harvey Bunter.

Although the crew were young and relatively new in the bank fishery, they had already gained enough skill to assist Captain Currie in keeping *Mack Mariner II* afloat and sound. On March 17, they managed to drop anchor in Sandy Cove, St. George's Bay. Two days later on Saturday March 19, the vessel was towed into the port of Stephenville by a tugboat used at the local paper mill.

The crew of the *Mack Mariner II* had finally reached safety, but that was not the case for the crew of the *Betty & Audrey.* Shortly after the towline broke on Wednesday, and the two vessels went their separate ways, Captain Banfield had decided to shorten up his canvas to just a small riding sail, and return to Port aux Basques.

Shortly after the crew was given the order, the schooner was hit by a huge wave that shook the *Betty & Audrey* and washed away the entire deck. Some of the crew managed to hang on, but twenty-two-year-old Clarence MacDonald of Gaultois was not so fortunate. He went over the side and was never seen again.

In one of the worst storms Captain Banfield had ever seen, there was little they could do to try and help their shipmate. In the icy water, the crew member, would have died in minutes.

The crew of the *Betty & Audrey* arrived in Port aux Basques and the loss of their shipmate was reported to his family back home. As for Captain Banfield, his time in the bank fishery was drawing to a close. Later that year, on December 29, 1949, the schooner and her crew were fishing near Dingwell, of the coast of Cape Breton, when a fire erupted and the vessel was totally destroyed.

From then on, Captain William Banfield took command of one more schooner named the MV *A & R Martin*. From there, he went in the coasting trade where he commanded the MV *Walter J. Sweeny* until he retired from the sea.

As for the *Mack Mariner II*, she remained in the fishery, and in 1952, she was put ashore at Port aux Basques and rebuilt by Norman Strickland, who removed her bowsprit, lengthened her eleven feet, and constructed a pilothouse aft. After being rebuilt, she was placed under the command of Captain Maxwell Currie of Rose Blanche until the late 1950s. During this time, she was used in the bank fishery and also for swordfishing.

In the late 1950s and the early 1960s, the *Mack Mariner II* had seen the last of her days in the fishery, and was now used to carry fish from Port aux Basques to North Sydney for her owner T. J. Hardy and Company Ltd.

On June 22, 1963, the *Mack Mariner II* departed North Sydney under the command of Captain Wilfred Keeping from Ramea. Her crew consisted of Austin Hardy and John Munden Jr. of Rose Blanche, and the captain's son, who was just a boy at the time.

The beginning of the voyage went uneventfully until the early-morning hours of June 23. While navigating in thick fog, the *Mack Mariner* went aground on Point Enragee, just four miles west of her destination of Channel, Port aux Basques. The sturdy old schooner was nearly refloated, but eventually declared a total loss.

Mishap at Sea: The Captain James Buffett Story

For the fishermen along the southwest coast of Newfoundland, leaving home and fishing out of the Cape Breton ports such as North Sydney and Glace Bay had become a routine way of life. The season out of Cape Breton ports ran from mid-spring until late December. James Buffett, from Rose Blanche, was one such young fisherman who left his home and family in Rose Blanche annually to fish the waters along Cape Breton Island.

James Buffett was born and raised in Rose Blanche and had started dory fishing as a young boy. By the early 1940s, he wanted his own skiff, so in 1944, he placed a order to the shipyard of Josiah Farrell in North Bay, La Poile, to have his own

James Buffett taken at North Sydney at the age of twenty-seven. (Photo courtesy of Dulcie Eavis).

skiff built. The next spring, when the ice cleared North Bay, the 47-foot MV *Dulcie Anne* was launched.

James became quite successful in the *Dulcie Anne* and continued to fish the winter months out of Rose Blanche and the remainder of the year out of Cape Breton ports. By the fall of 1948, James had fished for many seasons out of North Sydney. The fall of 1948 would be a little different for James and his wife Amelia, because, their only child, a daughter name Dulcie, was leaving home to work as a school-teacher in northern Newfoundland. This of course meant that when James left home to go fishing in Cape Breton, his wife would be home alone. As a result, James and his wife decided to relocate to North Sydney so they could spend more time together.

For the first couple of years, things went well for Captain Buffett and his wife in their new home, but it would not be long before that would change. By mid-June 1950, Captain Buffett and his crew had already made several trips to the fishing grounds and were preparing for another trip when crew member Kenneth LeMoine became ill and had to be hospitalized.

The crew were delayed for a few hours, but shortly before midnight on June 19, 1950, the *Dulcie Anne* departed North Sydney for the fishing grounds along the northern tip of Cape Breton. The vessel normally carried a crew of six and fished two dories, but this time they were one man short. The remaining five crew members were:

> James Buffett, captain, North Sydney
> Arthur Buffett , doryman, North Sydney
> John Hardy, cook, Rose Blanche
> Richard Piercy, doryman, Rose Blanche
> Arthur Billard, doryman, North Sydney

All went well on the departure, and the *Duclie Anne* arrived on the fishing grounds near Cape Smokey early the next day. The two dories were lowered over the side and the crew began to set their trawls.

Later that day, after the trawls were hauled back, and the catch not exactly plentiful, Captain Buffett decided to move further northward towards Cape North and St. Pauls Island. Upon arriving on the fishing grounds in the vicinity of Cape North, the weather was far from perfect so Buffett ordered the two dories to set four tubs of trawl per dory instead of the six tubs they normally used.

Shortly after the trawl was set, Captain Buffett encountered engine trouble. The *Dulcie Buffett* was powered by two gas engines, a 30-HP in the centre and a 20-HP on the quarter. The 20-HP, although just six months old, was the motor that was giving them trouble. Captain Buffett and his crew could finish the trip with one engine easily, but he still would have liked to have the other engine running as well.

By mid-afternoon, the weather had turned more favourable so Captain Buffett ordered the dories to set the remaining two tubs of trawl that were not set out that morning. After the trawl was set, the dorymen came back on board where Captain Buffett was still working on the motor. As the motor was just recently installed, Captain James Buffett was not that familiar with its components.

The crew however still had hope because crew member Richard Piercy was very familiar with this type of engine. Due to the fact that crew member Kenneth LeMoine was ashore sick, cook John Hardy had to join Arthur Billard in his dory. With this being the situation, the captain decided he would join his brother Arthur in the other dory while Richard worked on the engine.

The crew members boarded their dories and set out to retrieve their trawl. The first dory to row away carried James and Arthur Buffett, the second dory carried Arthur Billard and John Hardy. Back on board the *Dulcie Anne*, Richard Piercy was in the engineroom. Everything was going as planned.

The Buffett brothers were closest to the skiff, and shortly after they started retrieving their gear, Richard Piercy got the motor working. As the crew were retrieving the trawl, Richard Piercy steered the skiff close by with just one motor running and waited for the fishermen to off-load their catch.

As the *Dulcie Anne* was closing in on the dory, the engine had stalled again and Richard Piercy ran for the engineroom immediately with the hope of restarting it. However, he was unsuccessful.

The *Dulcie Anne* was still moving along erratically under the force of a riding sail (a small sail used to keep vessels steady when fishing) and was now heading straight toward the captain and his brother. On board the dory, the Buffett brothers tried to retrieve their trawl as fast as they could in the hope of having time to move the dory away from the quickly approaching skiff. However, they were not fast enough. The skiff and dory collided and a securing "eye bolt" on the stem, used when the vessel was rigged for swordfishing, hooked the gunwale of the small craft, capsizing it, and throwing the two brothers in the water.

Meanwhile, Richard Piercy was just coming back on deck from the engineroom when he observed the situation unfolding. He threw a life preserver attached to a rope to the brothers. They were fortunate enough to catch it, but Captain James Buffett could not hold on for long.

The second dory arrived on the scene shortly after and the two brothers were taken aboard the *Dulcie Anne*. Arthur Buffett was still conscious but James Buffett was not responding. The crew members took turns in carrying out first aid on the captain, but it was to no avail. He had already passed away.

For the shipmates of Captain James Buffett, the incident was far from over. Now they had the task of returning home with the body of a fellow shipmate, and reporting such a calamity to the families and authorities, is something that any shipmate fears.

The *Dulcie Anne* arrived back in North Sydney at 05:30 on June 21, 1950, and the accident was reported to the RCMP. The local doctor conducted an autopsy to confirm the cause of death.

A few days later, his body was taken to the funeral home in North Sydney, and buried in the local cemetery several days later. At the time of his death Captain Buffett was forty-seven years old. His wife continued to live in North Sydney and later remarried. Their only child Dulcie, continued to teach school and later moved the United States where she retired.

As for the *Duclie Anne,* she was sold in September of 1950 to William Sheppard of North Sydney. Then, in June 1957, she was sold to James Belliveau of Woods Harbour in southwestern Nova Scotia. There she was used mainly for the swordfishery and subsequently had several owners around Woods Harbour. Finally, in the late 1960s, the *Dulcie Anne* was put ashore and scrapped when the industry started to decline, and the new era of longliners were beginning to make their mark in the fishery.

The MV *Dulcie Anne* fishing off Nova Scotia in the 1950s.
(Photo courtesy of James Belliveau).

Collision in Port aux Basques Harbour

The port of Port aux Basques, on the southwest coast of Newfoundland, has been a busy harbour as long as history has been recorded. It was always a vital port for the many different aspects of shipping, whether it be the coastal trade, passenger ships, and/or the fishery.

When it came to the fishery, fishermen from a variety of places all along eastern Canada frequently called into Port aux Basques to fish for some sort of species or another over the years. This was due to the fact that the harbour itself is very close to the fishing grounds. During the winter of 1950, many fishing vessels and their crews had again made Port aux Basques their home port for the next several months until the weather improved and they could move further offshore.

February 19, 1950, was just another typical day on the fishing grounds on the southwest coast of Newfoundland. The weather was not ideal, but fishermen are no strangers to unfavourable weather conditions. At Port aux Basques, some men went fishing early and some remained docked a little longer. One of the skiffs still secured to the berth was the 46-foot MV *Man Alone*, under the command of Captain Edward Andrews of Francois.

Shortly after 05:00, the *Man Alone* departed her berth destined for the fishing grounds. Her crew consisted of cook Clifford Chant who was in the forecastle preparing breakfast, George Dollimount standing aft by the wheel, Norman Warren, George Warren, and Cecil Bowles were in the forecastle. The *Man Alone* carried one dory on deck and another in tow.

MV *Man Alone* being launched in North Sydney 1933.
(Photo courtesy of Alexander K. Ferguson).

As the *Man Alone* was leaving the harbour entrance, the 50-foot MV *George and Freeman* also of Francois, and under the command of Captain Henry Green, was approaching the dock inbound from the fishing grounds. The snow and darkness had reduced the visibility to nil. The two vessels were totally unaware of each other.

Within moments after leaving the dock, the skiffs collided. The bow of the *George and Freeman* struck the *Man Alone* just forward of amidships, damaging her planking all the way down to the water-line. The collision was devastating for the *Man Alone* and she sank within minutes.

The crew had to abandon the ship at once. They knew they only had one option and that was to abandon the skiff by the dory that was being towed. If they had not been towing the dory behind, they would have had to retreat to the water because they did not have time to launch the other dory. Shortly after they were on board their small craft, they were picked up the *George and Freeman*.

Now the *Man Alone* lay on the bottom of the harbour with just

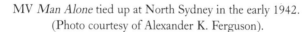

MV *Man Alone* tied up at North Sydney in the early 1942.
(Photo courtesy of Alexander K. Ferguson).

her spars above the surface. A local diver, named Nelson Kettle, from Grand Bay, later dove to the *Man Alone* in the hope of salvaging the skiff, but there was little success. Her spars were later removed and the bottom of Port aux Basques harbour was the destiny of the *Man Alone*. Her remains were never touched.

The MV *Man Alone* shortly after the collision in Port Aux Basques Harbour. (Author's Collection).

Crewman Lost From the Linda Diane

In the late 1950s, waterfronts in places along the Cape Breton coast had changed considerably. The skiffs and schooners were disappearing fast and the new longliners and trawlers were replacing the aging fleet.

The new and larger longliners had many advantages over the older skiffs and schooners. They had much more power, carried the latest navigational equipment, and required no dories. This of course meant that the fishing conditions were a little safer.

One of the first longliners to arrive in the town of North Sydney was the 58-foot MV *Linda Diane* which was built in Mahone Bay for

The MV *Linda Diane* shortly after being launched from the Maclean's Shipyard in Mahone Bay, Nova Scotia in 1954. (Photo courtesy of Linda Burke).

Captain George Kendall of North Sydney (formerly from Ramea). Captain Kendall fished for cod, halibut, swordfish, and his career on the *Linda Diane* was very successful. However, one trip on the *Linda Diane* would be remembered for a lifetime.

In November of 1956, Captain Kendall and his crew of John Hardy, Norman Vardy, George Lovell, and Percy Kendall (the captain's brother), were fishing for cod on Scatarie Bank off the Cape Breton coast. On the morning of November 24, the crew of the *Linda Diane* carried out their normal duties as they began to set their trawl. Once the trawl was out, they washed down the deck and went below for a short lunch. After several hours, Captain Kendall gave the order to get ready and retrieve the trawl.

Shortly after they began to haul back the lines, the wind began to increase from the northwest, a typical fall breeze off the coast of Cape Breton. As the crew continued to retrieve the gear, the wind also increased, so that by noon, the wind reached in the vicinity of forty knots. On board the *Linda Diane*, Captain Kendall and his crew tried their best to pull in the trawl as quickly as possible. The crew on board the boat was among some of the best longliner fishermen around and everyone knew their job well.

With the wind blowing strong, every man stood by his post. Captain Kendall was at the engine controls, Norman Vardy at the wheel, keeping the *Linda Diane* in her proper direction, George Lovell coiling the trawl, and John Hardy and Percy Kendall cleaning and storing the catch.

Just a short while later, the longliner was hit on the port side by a large wave, and the force of the wave caused the ship to list heavy to starboard. The list was large enough that water entered the slaughterhouse area, nearly filling it, right in the area the fishermen were working.

It is important to note that the deck of the *Linda Diane* was equipped with manholes. The manholes were used as an access hatch to below. On this occasion, one of the manhole covers was off, and a large volume of water had entered the vessel's fish hold. Yet, what was more tragic was that when the water began to flow out of the slaugh-

Percy Kendall on his wedding day in 1953. (Photo courtesy of Marcella Kendall).

terhouse area, Percy Kendall was forced out with it and into the cold frigid water of the Atlantic Ocean.

Captain Kendall tried to turn the longliner around in the hope of saving Percy, but the force from the sea locked the rudder in one position and the crew were unable to turn it. Just seconds later, Percy surfaced at the stern of the longliner, still alive, so one of the crew threw him one of the mooring lines. Luckily, Percy caught the rope on first attempt, but it was the very end, and he was unable to hold on. The end of the rope slipped through his hand and Percy Kendall disappeared beneath the surface.

Captain Kendall and John Hardy lowered a dory, praying Percy may surface again and that they would be able to get him. To their dismay, the dory was nearly swamped the moment it was launched.

The crew of the *Linda Diane* searched the area for hours, but his body was never found, hence, they returned to North Sydney to report the loss to his family. At the time, Percy left a wife and two children.

As for Captain Kendall, he continued to fish the *Linda Diane*, but several later years her fate was sealed as well.

In late August of 1959, the *Linda Diane* was returning from a

The MV *Ruth Lake* (Photo courtesy of Shipsearch Marine).

swordfishing trip off the coast of Nova Scotia. In the early morning hours of August 28, the vessel was approaching the coast of Cape Breton. Shortly before daybreak, the vessel became unstable due to a sudden ingress of water. Shortly after, the engine stalled.

Upon Captain Kendall's inspection of the engineroom, he discovered that the motor was half covered with water, and at once he gave the order to abandon the vessel in the two dories carried on deck. Little time was available to transmit a mayday and then abandon the sinking vessel, but somehow Kendall managed to do both.

The mayday was received by the local coast guard who notified the owners and other ships in the area. The owners notified another vessel in their fleet, the 57-foot longliner MV *Lenarfish* under command of Harold Keeping. The *Lenarfish* and the *Linda Diane* were coming home together, but early that morning, the *Lenarfish* stopped to transfer fuel.

The call for help was also picked by the bulk carrier MV *Ruth Lake*. The *Ruth Lake* was en route to Sept Iles, Quebec, and was not far from the *Linda Diane* at the time she was abandoned.

Later that day, the distressed fishermen were taken aboard the *Ruth Lake* and taken to the entrance of North Sydney Harbour where

they were transferred to the **RCMP** cutter. Her crew at the time of her sinking were:

George Kendall, North Sydney
Nathan Bernard, Rose Blanche
Eric Brown, Rose Blanche
John Hann, Isle Aux Morts
John W. Walters, Isle aux Morts
Job Williams, North Sydney

After the loss of the *Linda Diane*, Captain Kendall continued longlining and then took command of another vessel named the **MV** *Dorthea Reeves*. He commanded that vessel for the next several years, until the late 1960s, when he turned the command over to Captain Thomas Chislett. From there, Captain Kendall went to work on the local pilot boat. He passed away in the late 1970s.

The Wreck of the
Harry B. Nickerson III

In the beginning of the 1950s, North Sydney had become a booming port for both fishing vessels and commercial ships who visited to load coal and general supplies, along with the ferry service between North Sydney and Port aux Basques. Fishing began to increase when local fish merchants began to build and buy the newly designed longliners, mainly for the sword and halibut fishery off Canada's east coast.

The new fleet of longliners, did not only fish for sword and halibut. In the off-season, they also fished for greysole and cod, meaning the longliners fished nearly year round. This, along with the fact that many longliners from others areas often sold their catch at North Sydney, gave year-round work for the fish plants of North Sydney, and it was during these prosperous times, that many young fishermen and fish plant workers from the south and southwest coast of Newfoundland went to North Sydney.

All the young men who went seeking work quickly found it. Some stayed, while others returned back home when the work slowed down. In the fall of 1958, two young fishermen named George Hayman and Wilburn Rose from Rose Blanche, went to North Sydney to join the prosperous workforce. When they got there, they joined the crew of the longliner MV *Harry B. Nickerson III*.

The *Harry B. Nickerson III* was originally built in 1939, as the *A.J.P.*, and was named after her owner Almon J. Pack of East La Have, Nova Scotia. In 1956, she was purchased by N. B Nickerson and Sons Ltd., one of the leading firms in the fishery in Cape Breton at the time. Shortly after she was purchased, the Nickerson firm placed the longliner in the Marine Railway Dock at North Sydney. There the longliner was cut in two, near the midship section, and lengthened from sixty-five feet to seventy-six feet, and renamed the MV *Harry B. Nickerson III.*

In the fall of 1958, the *Harry B. Nickerson III* was preparing for a routine halibut trip to the western portion of the Grand Banks, in an area known as the Eastern Gully. In early November, the *Harry B. Nickerson III* departed North Sydney under the command of Captain Warren Levy of Liverpool, Nova Scotia. The destination was the Grand Banks, some 300 miles away. Her crew besides the captain were: Edward and Sidney Ingram (twin brothers from Burgeo, aged twenty-six), George Hayman (aged eighteen), Wilburn Rose (aged twenty-one from Rose Blanche), Murdock Barlett (aged thirty-six from Fortune), and Denton Scott (aged thirty-seven from Halifax).

The MV *Harry B. Nickerson III* tied up at Ingonish, Nova Scotia in 1956.
(Photo courtesy of John Bishop).

The voyage to the fishing grounds was uneventful, but shortly after arriving, the *Harry B. Nickerson III* and her crew were battered by strong winds and heavy seas.

On the morning of November 13, 1958, Captain Levy decided he would try and get a day of fishing, so early that morning, he ordered his crew on deck to bait the trawl. Shortly after 06:00, the *Harry B. Nickerson III* plunged into a huge wave, and the seams underneath her opened up. As a result, water began to ingress at a alarming rate.

At 06:25, the forward cabin began to flood and tables and chairs were afloat. Captain Levy sent his SOS and also contacted the long-liner MV *Robertson II*, under command of Captain Ches Abbott. Captain Levy then ordered the pumps manned and the crew to get the two dories ready.

A short while later, the crew abandoned the longliner into the dories. In the first dory was Edward Ingram, Wilburn Rose, George Hayman, and Murdock Bartlett. In the second was Captain Levy, Denton Scott, and Sidney Ingram. Before abandoning the longlin-er, Captain Levy radioed the *Robertson II* again and informed Captain Abbott that he would be anchoring the dories in the posi-tion he gave him on his previous call to expedite their chances of finding them.

Shortly after they abandoned the sinking longliner, and the dories were at anchor, the lines to the anchors had to be cut, because, as the weather worsened, Captain Levy feared that the dories would swamp. With the anchor lines cut, the dories stayed afloat, but were being tossed back and forth on the high seas of the Grand Banks. The first dory ran into some trouble when they lost one of their ores and was unable to retrieve it. Fortunately, Levy saw the incident and rowed to the dory and gave them another paddle.

Now the two dories were together and not far from the water-logged longliner. The two dories positioned themselves to the lee of the longliner to get a break from the seas. A little while later, Captain Levy boarded the sinking longliner again to check his position. By this time the fish hold was full of water and the forward deck was slightly submerged below the surface.

While on board the longliner, he ran to the bridge to check the radio. With power still to the bridge, he called the *Robertson II* again and updated them on their latest position. After doing this, he immediately boarded the dory once more.

Just ten minutes later, the engineroom bulkhead let go and the longliner sank within ten minutes some 100 miles south of Cape Pine, Newfoundland, and 275 miles east of Cape Breton. By now it was 09:00, and the *Robertson II* was just twenty miles away.

Finally the *Robertson II* arrived and picked up the distressed seaman in the two dories. Although they were shaken up, they all escaped without serious injury. Once on board, they were taken below to warm up and given something to eat.

At 15:00, on Saturday, November 15, 1958, the *Robertson II* arrived in North Sydney with the crew of the *Harry B. Nickerson III*, where families, friends, and company officials greeted them. Captain Levy first reported the loss of the longliner to her owners and then to the customs office. Several days later, George Hayman and Wilburn

The MV *Janet Irene* in Liverpool Harbour in the 1950s.
(Photo courtesy of Doug Levy).

Rose returned home to Rose Blanche while Captain Warren Levy and the engineer returned to their home in Nova Scotia along with the crew of the *Robertson II.*

Unfortunately, for Captain Warren Levy, his mishaps at sea were far from over, and the next time it would be more tragic. In January 1965, Captain Levy and his shipmate were on a short voyage aboard his 55-foot longliner MV *Janet Irene* when they were caught in a winter storm and the longliner was shipwrecked. Unfortunately, none of the three survived and only two bodies were found. Captain Levy was one of the two which was discovered a week later.

Captain Warren Levy's Headstone.
(Photo courtesy of Tim Mcdonald).

The Loss of Stanley Rose

By the late 1950s and the early 1960s in Newfoundland and Nova Scotia, the transition from the aging fleet of skiffs and schooners to modern longliners was almost complete. To many, it had seemed that the use for the once famous skiffs and schooners had come to an end.

However, just when it seemed that the end had come for the sturdy little crafts, it hadn't. Although many aging vessels were lying idle, and needed some minor repair, they had caught the eye of yachtsmen.

These yachtsmen knew that with a little repair and modification, they would make fine little pleasure crafts. There were a number of reasons why these boats were so attractive. First of all they were built strong to carry fish and coal etc. Secondly, they were built for long-term fishing excursions, hence they had accommodations for at least six people. The last, and probably most important reason, is because they were sold relatively cheap.

In the early 1960s, one such yachtsman and boat builder named James Rosborough from Nova Scotia, visited many parts of Newfoundland purchasing small skiffs known as "western" or "jack boats," taking them back to Nova Scotia for necessary repairs and alterations. During his visit, he came to ports along the southwest coast such as Port aux Basques, Rose Blanche, and Harbour Le Cou where he purchased several of these boats, one being the 49-foot, twenty-year-old, MV *Carolyn Marie* from the Buckland family in Harbour Le Cou.

James Rosbourgh returned to Port aux Basques regularly, and while on a visit in 1963, he came across another vessel he wanted to purchase, the MV *Lillian & Lizzie*. The 46-foot, twenty-year-old, *Lillian & Lizzie* was moored at the ferry dock in Port aux Basques and was owned by two brothers from Rose Blanche named Jacob and Theo Hatcher. The boat had been the brothers' home for several years.

At first, the brothers would not think of selling their boat simply because it was the only home they had. Thus they had refused to sell it on a number of occasions. Knowing this, James Rosbourgh offered the brothers a trailer along with some cash for the vessel. The brothers eventually agreed.

In the fall of 1963, James Rosborough returned to Newfoundland with the trailer and the agreement was carried out. The trailer was placed in their sister's backyard in Port aux Basques. The *Lillian & Lizzie* was then taken to Rose Blanche, and when James Rosbourgh returned to Nova Scotia, he sent a new motor back to replace the old one.

When the new motor arrived, it was installed, and the *Lillian & Lizzie* was ready for her new home. James Rosbourgh hired local seaman and handyman Stan Rose and a friend of Stan's named Alexander Knee. Both were no strangers to the sea. Stan had fished on these types of vessels before, and Alex had gone to sea on schooners at the age of seventeen while growing up in Badgers Quay, Newfoundland, He later joined the navy. Along with Alex and Stan were two crew members from Nova Scotia named Donald Holder and Cecil Thomas McMartin.

On Friday morning, November 29, 1963, the *Lillian & Lizzie* was moored at the dock in Rose Blanche. Stan waited for the lunch break at school to see his children before he departed on the voyage. Shortly after noon, the lines were slipped and the *Lillian & Lizzie* departed Rose Blanche. However, before she was to make the voyage to Nova Scotia, she was to have a brief stop in Port aux Basques for maintenance by a man named Garfield Piercy, a local welder.

Late that afternoon, and after the maintenance was finished, the *Lillian & Lizzie* departed Port aux Basques for Dingwell, Nova Scotia, on the northern tip of Cape Breton, the closest port to Newfoundland. From there, the crew planned to sail up the Bras d'Or Lakes and onward to Halifax.

Early that evening, they decided it would be best to top up the gas tank before the night came on. The gas had to be transferred from the barrels that were secured on the rail to the main gas tank, which was aft. After the gas was filled, Stan and Alex decided to go below for supper, before going on watch.

After supper was finished, Stan and Alex returned to the deck to relieve the crew member at the wheel; the other crew member was resting down below. When they arrived on deck, they noticed that the wind was increasing from the southeast and it was beginning to rain. Moments later, the *Lillian & Lizzie* was hit by a huge wave causing her to lurch to starboard.

At the time, the sails were hoisted and the engine was running. The force from such a wave caused the ballast to break loose and the vessel took a heavy list. The young seaman on the wheel managed to hold on and Alex Knee grabbed the hoops of the mainsail. Stan was not so lucky. He was washed off the deck and over the side in an instant and never seen again.

Everything happened so fast that they had barely time to hold on for their lives. The wave washed Stan over the side and ran down into the engineroom stalling the motor. With no engine and a list, there was little they could do with regards to searching for Rose.

Now the three seamen were left in the middle of the Cabot Strait with no engine and battered by winds and waves. Still they were blessed by a little fortune. With Alex Knee's previous experience in the navy as an engineer, he spent the night and next day taking apart the engine piece by piece. He then slowly, but surely, put the motor back together, drying each piece as he went. When it came time to start the engine, Alex knew his training had paid off. The engine started at once and they never experienced any trouble with it afterwards.

By this time ,it was late Saturday evening, and they were drifting for nearly a day. Because the wind was blowing from the east and southeast, while they carried out their repairs, the *Lillian & Lizzie* had drifted miles into the Gulf of St. Lawrence. When it was time to resume their voyage, they set course for Cape North, the very tip of Cape Breton, close to their original destination of Dingwell.

Stanley Rose taken at Rose Blanche in 1961.
(Photo courtesy of Gary Rose).

Finally, on Sunday, the vessel arrived in the port of Dingwell. Once they docked, the accident was reported to the police and the *Lillian & Lizzie* was left berthed at the wharf. Over the winter, she filled with water and sank. The next spring, she was refloated and taken ashore. After some repairs, she was towed to Ship Cove, near Halifax, by the MV *Mary J. Hardy*.

Although she finally reached her destination, her career as a yacht never took place. Later that year, she was cut into pieces and used as a chicken house.

As for Captain Stan Rose, his body was never found. At the time of his death he was forty-four years old. His wife Elizabeth, who was thirty-nine years old at the time, was left with seven children: Mary (twenty-one), Thelma (sixteen), Stanley (fourteen), Gary (twelve), Margaret and Marlene (eleven), and Sandra (seven).

The Storm of 1964

There are several stories commonly told amongst the fishermen along the south and southwest coasts of Newfoundland. These stories include the infamous *August Gales* and the *Southwest Coast Disaster* and are retold over and over because of the great loss of life that occurred. Another storm, which battered the coastline and fishing grounds off Newfoundland and Nova Scotia, occurred in December 1964. There were many lives lost from Quebec, Nova Scotia, and Newfoundland, and many of the survivors were battered. The following story entails several vessels involved in this storm, including the MV *Marie Carole*, MV *Cap David*, MV *Zerda*, MV *Zebu*, MV *Zibet*, MV *Red Diamond III*, MV *Eastern Pride*, MV *Jean & Judy*, MV *Cape Rock*, and the MV *Acadia Seahawk* to name a few.

In late November 1964, the *Cap David* and the *Marie Carole*, two 82-foot side trawlers, were taking on supplies in their home port of Cap aux Mueles, Ile De Les Madeleine, Quebec. The *Marie Carole* was the first to depart on the morning of November 30, under the command of Captain Alphonse Doyle. The *Cap David* departed the following morning on December 1, under the command of Captain Marcel Hubert. Both vessels were destined for the fishing grounds off the west coast of Cape Breton Island, near Cheticamp, approximately fifty miles away.

The *Marie Carole* arrived on the fishing grounds late on November 30 and the *Cap David* arrived the next day. The *Marie Carole* fished throughout the day of November 30, and after several hours of fishing on December 1, she departed the grounds near Cheticamp, and headed for Sable Island off the east coast of Nova Scotia, via the Canso Strait approximately 200 miles away.

The *Cap David* remained on the fishing grounds near Cheticamp. In the early afternoon of December 2, the wind began to blow from the southeast, and a slight sea began to build. Captain Hubert was observing this and knew the wind was likely to increase as the day wore on. Hence, he decided to take up the trawl net.

Captain Hubert's predication was correct. Shortly after commencing the retrieval of his trawl net, the wind was blowing at gale force. The crew of the *Cap David* were having difficulty securing the net and catch, and unfortunately things were about to get worse.

The *Cap David*, like most fishing boats, was equipped with what is known as a 'wash-down pump.' The pump supplies seawater to the main deck, where it is used for washing the fish, superstructures, and in some cases a fire line. The pump is located in the engine room and is driven by a belt from the main engine. While the vessel is engaged in fishing, the main engine is always running, therefore the pump is always supplied with power, and there is a constant water supply on deck for the crew. The pumping system on the *Cap David* was also fitted with a safety valve. The function of the safety valve was quite simple; if the hose leading from the pump to the deck became blocked, the valve in the engine room would open and the water would run down into the vessel's bilges where it would be pumped overboard by the bilge pump.

On board the *Cap David*, the pump was running as normal as the men worked hard to secure the net and stow the catch below. Unfortunately, the hose became kinked and the crew were too busy to notice. Moments later the safety valve opened.

While the men worked on deck, Captain Marcel Hubert remained in command on the bridge where he noticed some water being 'flicked' into the wheelhouse from the engine room. He immediately checked the engine room and discovered that the engine's flywheel was submerged in the water that was coming from the safety valve. He stopped the engine at once to avoid causing any further damage.

However, with the engine stopped, the bilge pump had no power. As a result, they couldn't pump the water out of the bilge and were now drifting around the Gulf of St. Lawrence with no power.

Preparing the MV *Cap David* for launching in June 1963 at Paspebiac, New Brunswick.
(Photo courtesy of the André Guévremont Collection).

Several hours before midnight, the wind changed to the southwest, but continued to blow at storm force. At the Canadian Coast Guard Station in Cap aux Meules, the winds were recorded at over eighty-five knots when the anemometer was blown completely off the building.

As the winds continued to blow, the crew of the *Cap David* began the task of bailing the water from the engine room, pail after pail. After a long and tiresome night, the men had removed most of the water. To avoid damaging the engine, they decided to change the oil in the base of the engine before restarting it.

Shortly after breakfast on the morning of December 3, the wind had changed to the northwest and began diminishing. The crew restarted the motor and set course for the port of North Sydney, where they arrived later that afternoon.

The *Cap David* was not the only vessel experiencing difficulty in the storm. The 86-foot trawler *Zerda*, under the command of Captain Harold Keeping, was fishing on Quero Bank, approximately eighty miles off the coast of Nova Scotia. Shortly before noon, on December 1, Captain Keeping decided to cease fishing after hearing the weather forecast and headed towards the port of North Sydney. Unfortunately, shortly after departing the fishing grounds, the oil pressure dropped in the main engine and the *Zerda* and her crew drifted helplessly for four hours.

At 17:00, the *Zerda* and her crew were still approximately twenty-five miles from the closest land mass which was Scaterie Island. The wind began to increase from the southeast, and the sea began to build. To make landfall, the *Zerda* would have to follow a northwesterly course, which meant the sea would be behind her. Early that evening, the seas began to wash over the deck of the *Zerda* causing damage to her rigging. At that point, Captain Keeping decided to turn the vessel into the wind where they rode out the storm all night.

The crew were taking a terrible beating. The *Zerda* had sleeping accommodations forward and aft, but to access the forward accommodations, the crew had to cross the open deck. With such poor weather conditions, Captain Keeping ordered the crew to stay where

The MV *Zerda*. (Maritime History Archives, Captain Harry Stone Collection).

they were. As a result, they had no contact with each other for approximately twenty-four hours.

Throughout the night and the next morning, the wind changed to the northwest and began to diminish. Captain Keeping set course for North Sydney and arrived there later that evening. The crew were exhausted, especially Captain Keeping, who stood at the wheel for fourteen hours during the peak of the storm.

Two more 85-foot side trawlers, the *Zebu*, under the command of Captain Ephriam MacDonald, out of Burnt Islands, Newfoundland, and the *Red Diamond III*, under command of Captain George Greene, out of Petite de Grau, Nova Scotia, were fishing on Quero Bank. They later departed the shallow waters of Quero Bank and headed for deeper water, hoping that the seas would diminish as the water got deeper. Their sister ship, the *Zibet*, under the command of Captain John W. Coleman, out of Isle aux Morts, had just arrived on Quero Bank that day, but decided not to commence fishing. Instead, they followed the same course of action as the *Zebu* and the *Red Diamond III*.

The MV *Red Diamond III* outbound Sydney Harbour in 1960.
(Photo courtesy of George Greene).

The next morning, when the wind changed to the northwest, the trawlers began to return to the fishing grounds, with the exception of the *Zibet*, which had to return to North Sydney to repair its depth sounder.

The *Zebu had* also experienced difficulties. As Captain MacDonald and his crew headed back to the fishing grounds, a wave hit the front of the trawler, breaking two wheelhouse windows, and subsequently flooding the wheelhouse and damaging the electronic equipment. The crew covered the windows with shutters, but the electronic equipment could not be repaired. This meant they had no communication with the outside world. However, Captain MacDonald still continued to fish.

The day continued on and there was no communications made with Captain MacDonald. As a result, it was believed something terrible had gone wrong. The crew themselves were the only ones who knew they were alright. Later that day, while having lunch in the galley, some of the crew were listening to a small transistor radio when it was broadcasted that their trawler was unheard of since the

The MV *Zebu* tied up at Burin after a trip on the Grand Banks in the early 1950s. (Photo courtesy of William Brushett).

storm and was now overdue. The crew immediately reported this to Captain MacDonald. In turn, he decided to call the trip off and returned to port. Early the next morning, the *Zebu* arrived in Isle aux Morts to off-load her catch and carry out much needed repairs.

Further westward, along the Nova Scotia fishing grounds, there were several other trawlers experiencing trouble. The 84-foot wooden stern trawler *Eastern Pride*, under the command of Captain Blackie Ross, was fishing on George's Bank when the storm struck. He immediately headed for deeper water, but at 10:00, on December 2, the vessel was hit by a huge wave that tore the wheelhouse off the main deck. Luckily no one was lost and only one of the crew members was injured. Along with the wheelhouse, went all the engine controls, and navigational equipment, including the compass. Now Captain Ross was left navigating his vessel with no controls, no compass, and no shelter.

Fortunately, Captain Ross gained valuable experience over the years. For three days he headed the *Eastern Pride* towards what he hoped was Halifax. Sure enough, on the third day, the stricken vessel arrived in Halifax. Her damage was estimated at 20,000 dollars.

Also fishing in the area near Sable Island was the wooden side trawler *Cape Rock*, under the command of Captain Floyd Gates. The *Cape Rock* was also hit by several huge waves, and the trawler suffered damage to some of her rigging and superstructure. Again the crew managed to repair what they could and got the trawler back to port.

All of the previously mentioned vessels were all affected by the same storm, but thankfully there were no lives lost. Fate would have a different plan for others.

Philman Quinlan and James Smith departed their home port of Stoney Island, Nova Scotia, on Monday, November 30, in their 38-foot lobster boat the MV *Jean & Judy* to set traps. The next morning, the two fishermen

The MV *Eastern Pride* at Port Greville in 1964.
(Photo courtesy of the Wagstaff Collection, Age of Sail Heritage Centre, Port Greville, Nova Scotia).

The MV *Cape Rock* at Port Bickerton in 1963. (Photo courtesy of Albert Fanning).

experienced engine trouble, and they anchored their boat just offshore to carry out the repairs. On December 1, when the storm

HMS *Cap De La Madeliene*, standing by the overturn hull of the MV *Jean & Judy*.

struck the area, the *Jean & Judy* tripped her anchor and was carried out to sea. Several vessels tried to offer assistance, but the seas were too high. Several days after the storm, the HMCS *Cap De La Madeliene* found the *Jean & Judy* overturned miles out to sea, but the bodies of the two fishermen were never found.

On the evening of December 1, the 125-foot steel side trawler *Acadia Seahawk*, owned by Acadia Seafood's of Mulgrave, Nova Scotia, was fishing in the vicinity of Sable Island under the command of a well-experienced captain named Ronald Mosher.

Several other vessels in the vicinity of the *Acadia Seahawk* heard her on the marine radio and everything seemed to be alright. However, during the night, something drastic must have occurred, because by morning, there was no sign of the vessel or her crew. Likewise, no radio contact was made. The *Acadia Seahawk* and her crew seemed to have vanished. The only wreckage ever found was discovered six months later along the shoreline in Port Hawkesbury, Nova Scotia. Several miles from the port the *Acadia Seahawk* last sailed, several teenage boys came upon an empty liferaft.

The MV *Acadia Seahawk* outbound for Mulgrave Harbour after annual refit *circa* 1960. (Photo courtesy of Albert Fanning).

At the time of her disappearance she carried a crew of fourteen. They were as follows:

Ronald Mosher, captain	Raymond Boudreau, seaman
Maxwell Dodge, mate	Tory Greencorn, seaman
Clayton Randell, 1st engineer	Wilson Dort, seaman
Gurth Mackenzie, 2nd engineer	Ted Boudreau, seaman
Simeon Lawrence, cook	Eric Fanning, seaman
Thomas Grant, seaman	Patrick O'Hearn, seaman
Jerome Boudreau, seaman	Wayne Granby, seaman

The *Acadia Seahawk* was not the only trawler to experience an unknown fate. The *Marie Carole* and her crew were fishing somewhere between Sable and Quero Bank when the storm hit the area. There was no radio contact made with the vessel and no wreckage belonging to her was ever found. There was some debris found east of Canso, but it was never confirmed as to which vessel it belonged to.

Captain Hubert of the *Cap David* thought he heard a call from Captain Doyle on the night of the storm, but he was not certain. The *Marie Carole* and her five-man crew were never heard from again. The crew of the *Marie Carole* on that fateful voyage were:

Alphonse Doyle
Redger Cyr
Rosaire La Pierre
Pierre Poirier
Edmond Richard

No one knows for certain what happened during the final hours, except for the fact that the *Acadia Seahawk* was known to have been fishing in the vicinity of West Point off Sable Island. This area is surrounded by shallow water known as West Point Bar. The sea floor in this area consists of sand, and when battered by high seas, the sea floor changes its contour. This is known as 'shifting sand.' Many

The MV *Marie Carole* in 1964
(Photo courtesy of The André Guévremont collection).

people feel that on the evening of December 1, when the storm first hit the area, the wind began to blow from the southeast and that the *Acadia Seahawk* was fishing to the southwest portion of the island. It is possible that maybe the *Marie Carole* was there as well, but no one knows for sure. If they were attempting to seek shelter, they would have likely rounded West Point to wait out the storm on the north side to get some sort of break from the wind and sea. As they attempted to cross the West Point Bar, they may have accidentally crossed over the shifting sand area, and capsized, as the sea broke in the shallow water.

Again this is only a presumption, and no one will ever know what happened in those final moments on that cold December night. Unfortunately, they will always be remembered by one terrible winter storm that raged the east coast of Canada, joining the long list of men lost at sea.

Adrift Aboard the Carroll Brothers

The summer fishery along the shore of Cape Breton was a prosperous place to be in the mid-1950s and 1960s. The waters along these shores were home to a variety of species of fish, making the ports of Glace Bay, Louisburg, North Sydney, and Ingonish, home to many visiting vessels

For many fishermen along the southwest coast of Newfoundland, the ports mentioned above were almost like a second home. Some of the fishermen visited these ports annually for nearly their entire fishing career.

One fisherman who knew these waters well was a resident of Fox Roost, Newfoundland, named Garfield Carroll. He had started fishing as a young lad in schooners and dories, and later resettled to Fox Roost. There, he and his wife raised a family, amongst them three strong and able sons. Garfield and his sons first fished in a small motor dory, but Garfield Carroll decided it was time for a bigger boat.

In the late 1950s, with this in mind, Carroll visited the shipbuilders at the yards in North Bay, La Poile, in the hope of placing a order to the builders for a new style of longliner. Fortunately, Garfield was in luck.

In the fall of 1960, the 38-foot MV *Carroll Brothers* was launched from the shipyard in North Bay, La Poile, built by master builder William Farrell.

The crew was quite successful in the new longliner, but it nearly ended in tragedy one fall day in a storm off the coast of Nova Scotia.

The MV *Carroll Brothers* at Margaree in 1965.
(Photo courtesy of Alvin Carroll).

It was late September 1965, and the *Carroll Brothers* arrived in Glace Bay for the annual fall fishing season off the coast of Cape Breton. On Saturday morning, September 19, 1965, the *Carroll Brothers* departed Glace Bay for the fishing grounds of Scaterie Island. Along with Garfield were his two sons, Alvin and Reginald. Late that afternoon, the crew of the *Carroll Brothers* experienced engine trouble and lost all radio contact with other fishing or commercial vessels in the area.

When the *Carroll Brothers* and her crew did not return to port by late Saturday evening, local residents and fishermen grew concerned. A few hours later, the fears grew worse when the folks on shore had seen flares out on the horizon in the vicinity were the longliner was fishing.

Immediately, the sightings were reported to the coast guard, and for the crew on the *Carroll Brothers*, it was about time. Things on board the longliner were growing worse, and by this point, the longliner was being battered by heavy seas and being carried out to sea by a strong offshore northwest wind.

The coast guard launched a search immediately, and throughout the night and early morning, the coast guard did indeed locate the distressed longliner. However, it could offer no help at the time due to the wind and sea conditions.

On Sunday morning, things seemed to improve when a heavily laden oil tanker came upon the *Carroll Brothers* and managed to make contact with the crew. The captain of the oil tanker offered help by wanting to tow the vessel close to the shore. However, the idea did not go as planned.

The *Carroll Brothers* as mentioned earlier, had no power and was not manoeuvrable when the oil tanker attempted to secure a towline. The bow of the *Carroll Brothers* got caught under the huge transom of the oil tanker, causing damage to her hull. Immediately the operation was abandoned.

Once the coast guard learned that an oil tanker had located the longliner for the second time, and was standing by, they sent the coast guard cutter MV *Sybella* to their aid. The *Sybella* arrived late that afternoon, and by this time, the winds and seas had abated. The coast guard ship was finally able get a towline to the longliner and the tow back to port began. Finally, at 19:30, Sunday night, the *Carroll Brothers* and her crew arrived back safely in Glace Bay.

The crew reported their ordeal back home to their families and commenced to carry out the repairs to their vessel. Although they had experienced a harrowing ordeal, they continued to fish for several more years until the boys decided to go into different trades. Alvin took the profession of driving trucks, while Reginald operated heavy equipment. Garfield Carroll, on the other hand, stayed with the sea, and five years later, experienced another close call.

In October 1970, he had signed on board an 85-foot coasting schooner named the MV *Sadie & Eva* under the command of Edward Anderson of Port aux Basques. Other members of the crew were George Anderson (the captain's brother), and Philip Bobbett, also of Port aux Basques.

On Tuesday, October 21, 1970, the *Sadie and Eva* departed Souris, PEI, partly loaded with vegetables. The next destination was North Sydney, where they were to load a part cargo of flour, and then journey on to Newfoundland.

At 05:00, on Thursday, October 23, 1970, the *Sadie and Eva* was about ten miles from North Sydney when a fire erupted in the engine-room. The captain sent a mayday and the crew abandoned the burning schooner and boarded the dory.

Fortunately, the mayday was received by two coast guard ships, the MV *Provo Wallis* and the MV *Rapid*. The *Provo Wallis* arrived on scene an hour and a half after receiving the mayday. They picked up the crew and then secured a towline to the burning schooner. The *Rapid* dispersed water to the burning schooner trying to salvage it. At 09:00, the *Sadie & Eva* arrived at the dock in North Sydney where the local fire department extinguished what was left of the blaze. She was later towed to Port aux Basques where she lies on a beach today.

The *Sadie & Eva* was the end of Garfield Carroll's career at sea. He passed away several years later at the age of sixty-seven.

Blackout Aboard the Zarp

In the late 1960s, the Newfoundland and Nova Scotia ports were becoming home to more and more trawlers as the otter trawl fleet steady increased. In Newfoundland, the larger trawler ports were places such as Marystown, Fortune, Grand Bank, Burgeo, and Harbour Breton.

Although the well-known fish firm of Fishery Products had most of their trawlers and plants in the larger ports, they still operated plants and trawlers in smaller ports as well, and the community of Isle aux Morts, located just east of Port Aux Basques, was one of them. The fish plant there was built in the mid-1940s, when the demand for fresh fish was on the rise.

Along with the plant, came two 85-foot trawlers called the MV *Zibet*, which was placed under the command of Captain James Chaulk, and the MV *Zebu*, which was commanded by Captain Ephraim MacDonald, both of Burnt Islands. The remaining crew also came from different communities along the southwest coast.

By the mid-1960s, Fishery Products was beginning to expand its fleet with new and larger stern trawlers. As a result, the *Zibet* and *Zebu* were sold back to the United States and they were replaced by two trawlers from Burin, named the MV *Zarp* and the MV *Zebra*. Both were 115-foot side trawlers that were built in Selby, England, in 1953, and came to Newfoundland in the late 1950s. The *Zarp* was placed under the command of Captain Ephraim MacDonald and the *Zebra* was placed under the command of Captain James Chaulk.

Both of the local captains were quite successful, but like any captain, it did not come without harrowing experiences and by battering many storms. The crew of the MV *Zarp* would experience one of these on a routine trip to the Grand Banks in the fall of 1966.

In late September 1966, Captain MacDonald and the crew of the *Zarp* departed their home port for a routine trip to the fishing grounds. Their destination was the Grand Banks to fish for flounder. The crew on this particular voyage was as follows:

Ephraim MacDonald, captain
Wilson Thorne, mate
John Wallace Coleman, 1st engineer
Cornelius Harvey, 2nd engineer
Charles Chant, cook
Hugh Keeping, deckhand

Earl Lawrence, deckhand
Israel Walters, deckhand
Frederick Thorne, deckhand
James Keeping, deckhand
George King, bosun

On Saturday, October 1, 1966, the *Zarp* had finished up her trip and was making her way back home to Burnt Islands, some 300 miles away. Late that morning, as the *Zarp* was passing the southwest portion of the Grand Banks, the engineer noticed that the main generator was not working properly and immediately notified the captain.

At once, the generator was stopped in the hope of carrying out the repairs, but in doing so, the crew were experiencing difficulty. The *Zarp* was equipped with an auxiliary generator, but it was not working either. As a result, there was no power supply for the navigational equipment and lights. The main engine was still running, but only on five of its six cylinders. Still the *Zarp* and her crew continued to make their way across the Grand Banks and towards home.

The waters which make up the famous fishing grounds of the Grand Banks and nearby

The MV *Fleetwood Lady*, sister-ship to the MV *Zarp*.
(Photo courtesy of the Bosun's Watch).

St. Pierre Bank, is the home to hundreds of fishing boats. It is also the shipping lanes for many of the commercial ships making their way to and from ports in Newfoundland, Nova Scotia, and the St. Lawrence Seaway. Captain MacDonald knew this and ordered the crew to raise its emergency navigational lights. By doing this, he hoped that other ships in the area would see them. The lights were 'lantern type" and burned fuel as its power source.

For the first few hours of their ordeal, no one knew that the *Zarp* or her crew were experiencing any kind of trouble. However, later on that day, when the owners could not contact the trawler, they became concerned.

On Saturday, October 2, an air and sea search commenced. Unfortunately, due to the heavy fog, efforts were hampered, and the search plane was forced to return to base. Back on board the *Zarp*, the engineers continued to work on the generator. Finally their hard work and skill paid off, as early the next morning, the generator was back in working order and all power was restored.

Once they had power, Captain MacDonald plotted his position and placed a call to the owners in Burin to notify them of his location and circumstances. The owners informed Captain MacDonald to divert to Burin and off-load his catch and carry out the necessary repairs.

Later that day, the *Zarp* arrived in Burin and discharged their fish. From there, they were sent to the Marine Railway Dock in North Sydney.

In the spring of 1967, the Fishery Products plant in Isle aux Morts closed, and the *Zarp* was taken to Paspebiac, New Brunswick. Captain MacDonald went on to command other fishing boats such as the MV *Gulf Gunn* out of Riverport, Nova Scotia.

After captaining the *Gulf Gunn*, MacDonald took command of a longliner named the MV *Pat & David* for three years, until he became captain of a herring carrier named the MV *Silver King II* which was owned by B. C. Packers Ltd. of Harbour Breton.

His command on board the *Silver King II* was very brief. He returned to the otter trawlers and then took command of a 55-foot wooden stern trawler named the MV *FLB 863-76*, which was owned by Eric King Fisheries Ltd. of Burnt Islands.

MacDonald's career in the *FLB 863-76* was successful to say the least, but on March 27, 1985, while fishing in the Cabot Strait, the trawler was damaged by ice and began to quickly take on water. The ingress of water was more than her pumps could keep up with and the crew abandoned the sinking trawler onto the ice. They were later picked by another fishing trawler, the *Blue Hake*, and taken to Port aux Basques.

Shortly after the sinking of the *FLB 863-76*, Captain MacDonald made several trips in another small trawler, but retired from the fishery shortly after. Today he resides in Burnt Islands with his wife.

The Wreck of the Zebra

When it comes to preserving the history of schooners, trawlers, fishermen, and the fishing industry along the southwest coast of Newfoundland, it would be nearly impossible without mentioning one person, Captain James Chaulk, known to everyone as "Chaulkie."

Captain Chaulk was born in Burnt Islands, to the son of George and Sidella Chaulk. Next to the house where James was born and raised, there was a fish plant, which was owned and operated by Monroe Limited and managed by James' father George. When James was old enough, he went to work with his father at the fish plant, and within a short time, took command of the *Dawnkist*, a 53-foot coasting schooner owned by Monroe.

After commanding the *Dawnkist* for several years, Captain Chaulk continued to work for Monroe, but instead of commanding schooners, he started captaining trawlers. The first trawler he took command of was the MV *Mustang*.

Apart from a brief break from the fishing industry in the 1950s, Chaulk captained trawlers for Monroe and later Fishery Products for nearly twenty years.

By the beginning of the 1960s, the Fishery Products' fleet began to grow quickly with the building of many large stern trawlers in the shipyards of Sorel, Quebec, and Bolnes, Holland. As more trawlers were being launched, the more men were needed to crew them.

In 1965, Captain Chaulk was in command of the 84-foot side trawler named the MV *Zibet*, but soon after, he was offered to captain the MV *Zebra*. Her former captain was William Brushett of Burin, but Captain Brushett had just joined the newly launched MV *Zeeland*.

The *Zebra* was a 115-foot side trawler built in Selby, England, in 1953. For the first three years of her career, she was operated by the St. Andrews Fish Company of Hull, England, under the name MV *St. Leonard*. Then, in November 1956, she was purchased by Fishery Products Limited of St. John's and brought to the port of Burin.

The fishermen that made up the crew of the *Zebra* with Captain Chaulk were from the Burnt Islands and the Isle aux Morts area. At the time, Fishery Products was operating a fish plant at Isle aux Morts and this was where the *Zebra* would off-load her catch. As the catch was being off-loaded, the crew would have an opportunity to spend some time with their families.

Captain Chaulk and his crew had great success in the *Zebra*, and in the fall of 1966, they were fishing for perch and cod in the Gulf of St. Lawrence around Ile De Les Madeleine. In late November of that

MV *St. Leonard* shortly after arriving in Newfoundland in 1956.
(Photo courtesy of William Brushett).

year, the *Zebra* arrived in Isle aux Morts with her hold full. After being off-loaded, the trawler was restocked with supplies for another trip to the fishing grounds. Her crew for the upcoming voyage consisted of:

James Chaulk, captain
Walter Bond, mate
Frederick Bryan, chief engineer
Joseph Savoury Jr., second engineer
Lloyd Lovell, cook
Harold Savoury, bosun

Theodore Thorne, deckhand
Reginald Hatcher, deckhand
David Seaward, deckhand
Emmanual Leamon, deckhand
William Kinslow, deckhand

In early December of 1966, the *Zebra* departed Isle aux Morts for the fishing grounds in the Gulf of St. Lawrence. The trip went well, and by late afternoon of December 11, 1966, the *Zebra* was again heavily laden with cod and perch. Early that evening, after the catch was stowed away and the deck secured, Captain Chaulk set course for the port of Isle aux Morts.

As the *Zebra* got under way, Captain Chaulk stood watch on the bridge as the crew worked away on deck repairing the net. The wind was blowing from the southwest which caused the trawler to roll from side to side. The rolling caused a slight discomfort for the crew on deck, but it was nothing they hadn't experienced before. Back aft in the galley, dishes and other items were being thrown around as the *Zebra* and her crew made their way home.

Shortly after midnight, the weather began to improve and Cook Lloyd Lovell went to work cleaning up the galley. At 04:00, the watch changed, and Mate Walter Bond took over the conduct of *Zebra*.

About 05:00, on December 12, 1966, the *Zebra* was approaching the eastern entrance to Isle aux Morts harbour. The wind was still blowing from the southwest and the sea was gradually building from the long fetch of the wind. The visibility was fair and the temperature near zero degrees celsius. Captain Chaulk was on the bridge in command and Mate Walter Bond was at the wheel.

At 05:30, near Fish Point, things would change when the crew of the *Zebra* felt a large thump and soon discovered that she had hit bottom. Although, at the time, the trawler was steaming at a slow speed, she was heavily laden and the momentum of the impact shook the trawler greatly. The *Zebra* suffered immense damage and began to take on water immediately, which resulted in a fast list to port.

With less than ideal weather conditions, the situation grew dangerous quickly, and Captain Chaulk ordered the crew to don their lifejackets. Shortly after going aground, the *Zebra* broke in two, and the forward section sank. The wheelhouse and aft deck remained on the rocks, listed to port, and awash by the sea.

The *Zebra* carried three dories on the aft deck and Captain Chaulk ordered the crew to ready them all. Shortly after the dories were untied from their cradles, a sea washed over the afterdeck of the *Zebra,* carrying way all three dories, and beating them into pieces.

The vessel was also equipped with two liferafts, but the sea carried one of them away as well. They managed to grab onto the one remaining and decided to inflate it on deck. Moments after pulling the inflation cord, the liferaft hooked the davit, and would not inflate.

Now the crew were standing on the deck of a wrecked trawler, being constantly washed by the sea in total darkness. The one remaining liferaft which was partially inflated was of no use because it didn't have enough air to keep any of the crew afloat. The only life-saving equipment they had was the lifejackets they were wearing.

Back on land in Isle aux Morts, local resident Norman Lefrense and his son Alexander had awakened shortly before daylight. They were planning a trip to nearby Otter Bay. As Norman and his son were having breakfast, they noticed a light near the eastern entrance to the harbour, but made nothing of it, thinking it was one of the local fisherman.

After breakfast, Norman and Alexander boarded their 16-foot motorboat and started on their trip. However, shortly after leaving the dock, they noticed oil in the harbour, and immediately speculated that throughout the night, something must have gone wrong.

Within minutes of leaving the wharf, they soon found out

where the oil was coming from when they saw the aft deck and wheelhouse of the *Zebra*. Another fisherman from Isle aux Morts, John William Walters was already at the scene of the wreck. He discovered the distressed fisherman a little while earlier when he went to check his nets. John William Walters had already taken half of the crew on board his boat, but could take no more for fear of overloading it.

Now Norman and his son started the task of taking the remaining crew off. Captain Chaulk experienced a narrow escape himself. He was still in the wheelhouse when the trawler listed to port and he slid across the wheelhouse. Luckily the wheelhouse of the *Zebra* had wooden grating on its deck. Chaulk managed to hook his finger in the holes of the grating and somehow managed to crawl back to the starboard side. He then exited the wheelhouse through the door on the starboard side and onto the aft deck where he stood with the remainder of the crew trying to abandon the sinking trawler.

When Captain Chaulk finally got on deck, he helped the remaining crew aboard the motorboat of Norman Lefrense. The last two crew members left aboard the *Zebra* were Captain Chaulk and Cook Lloyd Lovell. Lloyd, who had been up the best part of the night cleaning the galley, was lightly dressed as he had just gotten into his bunk before the grounding occurred. Lloyd Lovell managed to grab onto the rail on the aft deck.

Finally, Captain Chaulk, along with Norman and Alexander Lefrense, managed to get Lloyd aboard the motorboat. By this time, the cold temperature was beginning to take its toll on the young seaman.

At 08:30, after three hours of being wet and cold, the shipwrecked crew members arrived at the wharf in Isle aux Morts. They were quickly taken to homes of local residents, with the exception of Lloyd Lovell, who was immediately taken to the hospital.

Although they had a narrow escape, all of the crew managed to survive, with the exception of twenty-seven-year-old Lloyd Lovell. He passed away before reaching the hospital. He left behind his wife Mary Jane, aged twenty-two and five children: Cythina (aged five),

Lloyd Lovell and his wife Mary Jane, on their wedding day, August 17, 1961. Seated directly below Mary Jane, is John Billard. (Photo courtesy of Cynthia Harris).

Verna (aged four), Lloyd Jr. (aged three), Greg (nineteen months), and Debbie (four months).

Not long after the sinking of the *Zebra*, Norman Lefrense, Alexander Lefrense, and John William Walters, were awarded a medal of bravery for saving the crew of the wrecked trawler that cold and terrible night.

Receiving Medals of Bravery at Port aux Basques. (L-R) Norman Lefrense, John William Walters, Magistrate Lloyd Wicks, Alexander Lefrense, and Captain James Chaulk.
(Photo courtesy of Alexander Lefrense).

Collision in Halifax Harbour

The fishing community of Glace Bay, on the coastline of Cape Breton, has always been a popular port for fishermen from Newfoundland and other parts of Nova Scotia. These men came to fish for cod, swordfish, greysole, lobster, and other species. As a result, the harbour of Glace Bay was often filled with longliners from early spring until late fall.

The fishermen of Glace Bay saw a change in the late 1950s, as well as other Nova Scotia fishing ports, with the introduction of the new type of longliners, and from April to July, four new longliners arrived in Glace Bay. They were MV *Alice & Rita*, MV *Elizabeth & Leonard*, MV *Arthur Ross*, and MV *Sea Breeze 4*.

All four vessels were sister ships and were built at the shipyard of A. F. Theriault and Sons in Meteghan River, Nova Scotia. On April 23, 1957, *Sea Breeze 4* was the first of the four to be launched. The longliner measured fifty-seven feet in length, seventeen feet two inches beam, and was powered by a 150-horsepower six cylinder Leland diesel engine. Her owner and operator was Captain Joseph Wilneff of Glace Bay.

The *Sea Breeze 4*, like the rest of the new longliners, was designed to fish for halibut, swordfish, and cod. These types of fish, required long trips far away from home, and much of the time, inclement weather. The new vessels would provide the fishermen with more comfort and safety.

Cod and halibut were caught during the winter and spring, while swordfish was caught during the summer and fall. In the spring of 1958, many longliners from both Newfoundland and Nova Scotia, including the *Sea Breeze 4*, were fishing for cod on the west coast of Newfoundland in the vicinity of Bay St. George. The catch rates were good and they were on a load and go basis.

In early May of 1958, the *Sea Breeze 4* arrived in Glace Bay, heavily laden with cod after her first trip to the fishing grounds. After the catch was off-loaded, and a short stay at home, the crew of the *Sea Breeze 4* were ready to leave again. On the evening of May 8, 1958, the vessel again departed Glace Bay, for the fishing grounds of Bay St. George, some 110 miles away.

The beginning of the trip was uneventful, but shortly before dawn on May 9, 1958, the vessel struck a blanket of dense fog as she neared the coastline of Newfoundland. As daylight approached, the *Sea Breeze 4* was just beginning to come to the entrance to St. George's Bay when the crew heard a loud thump. Captain Wilneff ran to the wheelhouse to investigate and soon discovered that they had gone aground at Cape Ray, just below the lighthouse.

Although it was foggy, the wind and sea was light, so the crew had no trouble abandoning the longliner.

Captain Wilneff reported the incident to the proper authorities and returned home. Within no time, the rigging was stripped and a hole cut in her side to remove the engine. Not long afterward, the *Sea Breeze 4* was declared a total loss.

Although it appeared that the *Sea Breeze 4* had a short career, there was still hope for the new longliner. A local fish merchant named T. J. Hardy from Port aux Basques had heard about the grounding from her owner. A short while later, he decided to go to the scene of the wreck and see what damage the vessel had actually sustained.

When Mr. Hardy arrived at the wreck site, he was somewhat surprised. Although the *Sea Breeze 4* was hard aground, the only damage she suffered was to her keel, some broken planks, and a hole cut in the portside where someone had removed the engine. Mr. Hardy had spent a lifetime around boats and knew that the *Sea Breeze 4* could still be used in the fishery with a little repair.

A short while later, Mr. Hardy purchased the wreck and had the

The MV *Sea Breeze 4* aground at Cape Ray in May 1958. (Author's Collection).

hole in the port side temporarily repaired. Then the hull of the *Sea Breeze 4* was towed off the rocks and taken to Port aux Basques where she was hauled ashore near Mr. Hardy's fish plant. Then a carpenter, and long-time friend named Norman Strickland, started on the repairs. After a short while, they had installed a new keel, timbers, planks, spars, rigging, and the original engine. It was now late fall and the longliner was ready for fishing again. She was renamed the MV *Mack Mariner III* and placed under the command of Captain Maxwell Currie of Port aux Basques.

The *Mack Mariner III* fished for the next few years in the cod, halibut, and swordfisheries. During these years, the vessel had a very successful career. Along with the success, the vessel had experienced some very inclement weather, but always survived. One of the worst storms was in April of 1963, when a ferocious storm whipped through the Gulf of St. Lawrence. The *Mack Mariner III*, along with several

The MV *Mack Mariner III* tied up in Port aux Basques in 1965.
(Maritime History Archives, Captain Harry Stone Collection).

other vessels survived, but her sister ship, MV *Elizabeth & Leonard*, under command of Frederick Oates of Glace Bay, was lost with all hands.

Although the *Mack Mariner III* had survived many storms and her first mishap at sea, her career did not last very long. In the spring of 1968, the *Mack Mariner III* was swordfishing off the coast of Nova Scotia, and under the command of Edwin Hardy Jr. of Rose Blanche. Her crew consisted of Lesley Currie, George MacDonald, Joseph Ingram, Frederick McNeil, and Thomas Taylor.

In mid-June, the *Mack Mariner III* had arrived in Halifax to off-load her catch. Once the catch was unloaded, the stores were restocked and vessel was ready for fishing again.

On the evening of June 22, 1968, she departed Halifax for the fishing grounds known as Western Banks (just west of Sable Island). The weather was clear and the winds were fair.

At 21:00, *the Mack Mariner III* was outbound Halifax Harbour at Chebucto Head. Also outbound at the time was another longliner, the 84-foot MV *Margaret R.M. II*, under command of Isaac Bullen, also destined for the fishing grounds.

A few moments later, the two boats collided, damaging the amidships section of the *Mack Mariner III*. The bow of the *Margaret R.M. II* had also hit the wire stay going from the mainmast to the foremast, breaking off the two spars.

The *Mack Mariner III* sank by the stern immediately, leaving the crew with just enough time to board the *Margaret R.M. II*. The longliner sank until only a small section of her bow remained above the surface.

Seeing that the *Mack Mariner III* was remaining afloat, an attempt was made by the *Margaret R.M. II* to tow the disabled vessel back to Halifax Harbour. The bowline of the *Mack Mariner III* was secured to the *Margaret R.M. II* and the tow effort began.

However, within thirty minutes, the *Mack Mariner III* began to sink a little more, until finally, there was nothing above the surface. By

The MV *Margaret R.M. II* at Meteghan River, Nova Scotia in 1964, shortly after being launched. (Photo courtesy of Chelsea Miles).

now it was dark and the towrope was released for safety reasons. As a result, the *Mack Mariner III* slowly sank to the bottom of Halifax Harbour. The crew were taken back to Halifax and later returned home by the CN Ferry.

Collision in the Cabot Strait

From the mid-1960s to the early 1970s, the waters from the Avalon Peninsula westward, along the southwest coast of Newfoundland, into the Cabot Strait and the Gulf of St. Lawrence had experienced a sudden increase in herring stocks. Before this time, the species was mainly used for baiting trawls and lobster traps. However, with its sudden rise in stocks, its demand increased as a commercial fishery.

Herring travel in schools, and like many other fish, follow certain migratory patterns and concentrate in certain areas. Most often they stay close to the surface, which means that the only way to catch them is to extend the net from the surface downward. Once the herring entered the net, the bottom portion is closed and brought to the top. This type of net is known as a purse seine.

The fishermen along the south and southwest coast of Newfoundland had lots of experience fishing herring, but not catching them in such huge amounts or in such a technique. The only seiners owned in Newfoundland in the 1960s were on the west coast, where the herring fishery had been popular for the last sixty or so years. In order to keep up with the demand for herring, experienced seiners and fishermen from Nova Scotia, British Columbia, and New Brunswick, came to the waters of Newfoundland. The result was that these waters were the homes of dozens of seiners who fished in areas from the Gulf of St. Lawrence to every little inlet that had room to purse a seine. Like the waters in other areas, these were also used by other ships with a different purpose. It was also the shipping lanes for hundreds of commercial ships on routine trips to and from the European ports destined for ports in Quebec and the Great Lakes.

Ships destined for ports in Quebec and the Great Lakes must enter the Gulf of St. Lawrence, either by the Strait of Belle Isle, between Labrador and Newfoundland, or through the Cabot Strait, between Newfoundland and Cape Breton. The entrance of the Strait of Belle Isle, is not navigable by most ships from December to early June because of ice, so the entrance at the Cabot Strait is the only alternative.

The spring of 1969 was the start of another peak year for the herring fishery in the Gulf of St. Lawrence, and seiners from all over were continuously returning to port fully ladened with herring. One of the vessels making up the fleet in the spring of 1969 was the MV *Melissa Jean II*. The *Melissa Jean II* was a newcomer to the herring fishery as she was launched just the previous July from the yard of A.F. Theirault in Meteghan, Nova Scotia. The 102-foot seiner was owned by Keith Raymond of Centerville, Nova Scotia, and carried the most recent navigational equipment.

On the morning of April 27, 1969, the *Melissa Jean II* was under the command of Glendon Outhouse of White Head, Grand Manan Island, New Brunswick. The vessel was fishing in the vicinity of the Madeleine Islands and was fully loaded with herring, destined for the port of Isle aux Morts.

Shortly after midnight, the seiner was approaching the Cabot Strait near Channel Head, Newfoundland. Not far from the *Melissa Jean II*, and approaching the Cabot Strait from the seaward, was the 4,200-ton Israeli general cargo ship, MV *Eshkol* owned by Zim Lines. The *Eshkol* was a regular visitor to St. Lawrence and the Great Lakes ports.

Early in the morning of April 27, 1969, the two vessels were navigating in close proximity, and shortly after midnight, a collision occurred between the two vessels. At 01:24 ADT, the master of the *Eskhol* made a call to Sydney Coast Guard Centre, informing them that his ship had collided with a fishing vessel and they were searching for survivors.

The *Eshkol* was a steel constructed general cargo ship and fitted with a clipper style bow. The sharp bow of the *Eskhol* had struck the *Melissa Jean II* in the midship section. This section sank immediately, but the bow section remained afloat. Consequently, the crew members tried to abandon the sinking seiner as fast as they could.

The MV *Eskhol* in the Welland Canal in 1972. (Photo courtesy of Brian Bluekamp).

The collision was not only drastic for the *Melissa Jean II*, but it was also dreadful for her crew. Crew members Paul Morse and David Guptil, who were in the forward cabin below, had managed to survive

MV *Melissa Jean II* at Meteghan River, NS, in 1968.
(Photo courtesy of Juanita Trecartin).

Stanley Currie at Port Aux Basques in 1967.
(Photo courtesy of Annie Buckland).

LIST OF THOSE LOST

Glendon Outhouse, aged 41,
White Head Island, NB
Clifford Newman, aged 38,
White Head Island, NB
Larry Trecartin, aged 27,
White Head Island, NB
Stanley Currie, aged 23,
Port aux Basques, NL
Terry Osmond, aged 18,
Port aux Basques, NL

the collision, and were taken aboard the seiner MV *Atlantic Harvester*, who later took them to Port aux Basques. Other vessels continued to search the area, and a little while later, the body of thirty-nine-year-old Gordon Locke of Grand Manan, New Brunswick, was found by the seiner MV *Stewart Lynn*. His body was then taken to Port aux Basques as well.

Although ships continued to search the area in the hope of finding other survivors, or even their bodies, they couldn't find any. The bodies of the remaining crew members were never found.

Just two weeks after the collision, the bow section of the *Melissa Jean II*, which remained afloat, drifted ashore on a beach near Gabarus Bay, Cape Breton Island. The wreckage was

Larry Trecartin during Christmas 1968.
(Photo courtesy of Juanita Trecartin).

Two views of the bow of the MV *Melissa Jean II* at Gabarus Bay, NS, in May 1969. (Wallace Currie photos).

searched in the hope of finding some of the crewmen's bodies, but there was nothing except several items of clothing hanging from their hooks.

Not long after the collision, a monument was erected overlooking White Head Island in memory of the crew of the *Melissa Jean II*.

The monument in memory of the MV *Melissa Jean II* and her crew overlooking White Head Island, Grand Manan Island. (Photo courtesy of Thiry Morse).

The Wreck of the Eastcliffe Hall

The Great Lakes and St. Lawrence Seaway is a system of lakes and canals that make up the longest inland waterway system in the world. The seaway begins in Montreal, at St. Lambert Lock, and from there, vessels can travel westward some 1,000 nautical miles over five major lakes, and travel west as far to ports such as Thunder Bay, Superior, and Chicago.

To reach such ports, and to cover such a distance, these ships must navigate many confined rivers and channels. Over the years, thousands of ships of a variety of sizes and types have transited these waters from all over the world, carrying almost any type of a cargo you can imagine.

With such large numbers of ships over such a long period of time, mishaps, accidents, shipwrecks, and tragedies are inevitable. One of the more recent shipwrecks in the St. Lawrence Seaway was the bulk carrier MV *Eastcliffe Hall.*

The *Eastcliffe Hall* was a 254-foot diesel-powdered freighter built in 1954 for the Hall Corporation at the Canadian Vickers Shipyard in Montreal. In 1959, when the new St. Lawrence Seaway was opened, and much larger ships could transit the lock and canals, the *Eastcliffe Hall* was lengthened to 343 feet.

The *Eastcliffe Hall* was built to carry cargoes such as grain, pulpwood, and coal. However, in the summer of 1970, the *Eastcliffe Hall* was chartered to carry "Pig Iron" from Sorel, Quebec, to ports on the Great Lakes. On July 13, 1970, the freighter was transiting the locks and canals of the Montreal-Lake Ontario section of the St. Lawrence Seaway. The crew making up this particular voyage were:

Captain Richard Albert Groulx, Montreal, QC
Chief Officer Julien Marchand, Champlain, QC
Third Officer Joseph Dupuis, Midland, ON
A/B Patrick Collins, St. Catherines, ON
A/B Samuel Young, Ramea, NL
A/B Freeman Barter, Ramea, NL
O/S Edwin Fudge, Ramea, NL
O/S Gordon Ball, Ramea, NL
O/S Gordon Crewe, Ramea, NL
O/S Donald MacDonald, Ramea, NL
Chief Engineer William Demers, Charlesbourg, QC
Second Engineer Marcel Gendron, Batiscan, QC
Third Engineer John Scott, Montreal, QC
Fourth Engineer Leonard Harris, New Chelsea, NL
Mechanical Assistant Melvin Harris, Burnt Islands, NL
Chief Cook Louis Boucher, Montreal, QC
Second Cook Lawrence MacDougall, Kentville, NS
Porter Walter Durmuller, Niagara On Lake, ON

The MV *Eastcliffe Hall* in the Welland Canal in 1963.
(David Glick photo – Brian Bluekamp Collection).

Also on board at the time was the captain's sixteen-year-old son Alan Groulx, Jacqueline Demers, wife of the Chief Engineer, along with their six-year-old daughter Natalie.

The living accommodations on board the *Eastcliffe Hall* was similar to many of the vessels built for the Great Lakes with the navigation bridge located forward. The decks below the bridge were cabins for the captain, deck officers, able seamen, and ordinary seamen. The engineroom and galley was located aft, along with the cabins for the crew of these two departments.

The crew of the freighter worked on a three-watch-system. It consisted of four hours of work followed by an eight hour rest period. The schedule of watches ran from 12-4, 4-8, and 8-12 twice daily.

Shortly before 04:00, on July 14, 1970, the 12-4 watch was relieved by the 4-8 watch. Samuel Young was the 12-4 A/B. After leaving the bridge, he went directly to his cabin. Shortly after, the crew of the *Eastcliffe Hall* felt a loud thump, and moments later, another thump was felt, followed by rushing water and crashing steel.

The crew soon discovered that the freighter had hit bottom on Chrysler Shoal. Samuel Young was still awake and knew something had gone wrong. He immediately woke the remaining crew sleeping in the forward accommodations.

As the crew grabbed their lifejackets, they hurried for the lifeboats which were located aft on the boat deck. The *Eastcliffe Hall* began to fill with water and was sinking quickly by the bow. As the bow sank, the stern began to rise, causing difficulty for the crew to make their way aft and lower the lifeboats.

Eventually, the forward crew made their way aft, but by this time, the freighter was trimmed excessively by the bow, and the crew slipped off the deck and into the water. After falling into the water, the crew had to battle against the suction of the sinking ship which kept pulling them beneath the surface. They grabbed onto anything they could find and some of them even tied themselves together. They drifted some distance downriver before being picked up.

Of the twenty-one crew and passengers on board, twelve were lucky enough to be rescued, but nine others lost their lives including

Captain Groulx and his son, Chief Engineer William Demers, along with wife and daughter, Lawrence MacDougall, Leonard Harris, Freeman Barter, and Louis Boucher.

As for the *Eastcliffe Hall*, she was later dynamited and today is often visited by scuba divers.

The Vair

In the mid-1960s, the new technique of longlining for swordfish had just been introduced to the fishermen of Newfoundland and Nova Scotia. The days of harpooning them, and standing for hours on the "for top" scanning the horizon, had come to an end.

During the days of swordfishing, the ports along the coastline of Cape Breton such as North Sydney, Glace Bay, Louisburg, and Ingonish had become very popular. This was because of several reasons. First of all, swordfish always stayed in warm water, and this of course kept them closer to Nova Scotia's coast than to Newfoundland's. Secondly, the ports were relatively close to the fishing grounds. Third, there were several large fish firms located there that operated longliners in the swordfishery, and paid good prices for the catch.

One of the better-known firms that owned and operated a fleet of longliners, along with a large fish plant, was the firm of H. B. Nickerson's and Sons Limited. They were based in North Sydney, and in the early 1950s, they began to purchase some of the first newly designed longliners. Throughout the 1950s, they continued to increase their fleet with longliners ranging from fifty-five to seventy-five feet in length.

In order to keep the fleet fishing, the firm needed captains and crews. Consequently, in 1957, they hired a young captain from Port aux Basques named Maxwell Currie.

Although Maxwell Currie was only twenty-seven at the time, he had already been at sea for thirteen years; five of them as master. His first trip as a doryman was aboard the 51-foot skiff from Rose Blanche named the MV *Justrite*, under command of Jacob Bartlett. Three years later, he signed on board a six-dory banker named the MV *Jane Robert* under Captain Leonard Broydell. Several years later, at the age of twenty-two, he was given his first command, the four-dory, 64-foot schooner named the MV *Mack Mariner II*, which was owned by T. J. Hardy and Company Ltd. of Port aux Basques.

For the Nickerson firm, Captain Currie's first command was a 75-foot longliner MV *Harry B. Nickerson*. For the next nine years, he captained several of their longliners such as the MV *Elaine Judith*, MV *Betty Harris*, and the MV *Nancy N*. By 1966, Currie had become quite successful commanding longliners, especially fishing for halibut and swordfish. He spent most of his time in charge of the *Nancy N*, but because of his success, the firm wanted a newer and bigger longliner for Currie and his crew.

The MV *Nancy N* docked at Port aux Basques heavily laden with cod and halibut after a trip in the Gulf of St. Lawrence in March 1966. (Photo courtesy of Maxwell Currie).

The Nickerson firm gave Captain Currie the task of drawing up plans for an 85-foot longliner. It didn't take long before the captain had the plans he wanted, and shortly after, he went to Boston to discuss the blueprints with a naval architect named John W. Gilbert. The plans were approved, and the contract to build the new longliner was put in place.

The building contract was awarded to Atlantic Shipbuilding Ltd. in Mahone Bay, Nova Scotia. Although the original plans indicated that the longliner was to be eighty-five feet in length, the keel was longer than they needed so they installed several more frames and extended her length to ninety-one feet. The construction went well, and in November of 1966, the 149-ton MV *Vair* was launched. The longliner carried the latest in navigational equipment such as two radars, two sounders, autopilot, Loran A, Loran 9, two radio telephones, and was powered by a V16 GM engine.

The MV *Vair* in Mahone Bay in 1966. (Photo courtesy of Maxwell Currie).

On January 16, 1967, Captain Currie and his crew were ready for their maiden voyage, and departed North Sydney for a halibut trip to the Grand Banks. The *Vair* proved to be a fine vessel and everything went well.

However, it would not be until the second trip in late February that the *Vair* was really put to the test. Again they were fishing for halibut on the Grand Banks when the fishing grounds were battered by a raging winter storm.

Although the longliner and her crew had managed to survive, that was not the case for some of the other vessels. The 78-foot schooner/longliner MV *Maureen & Michael* was struck by a huge wave which damaged the superstructure amidships. Its slaughterhouse was made fast to the 6" x 6" stanchions that came up through the deck, and after the house was carried away, the vessel began to take water down through the stanchions which had opened up.

Fortunately, the crew of the *Maureen & Michael* were rescued, but that was not the case for the crew of the 85-foot *Polly & Robbie*, under the command of Captain Edwin Brewer of Lockeport, Nova Scotia. He was lost, along with his entire crew, and the only thing that was found was a portion of the wheelhouse.

Although it had been a rough winter, the crew battered the weather, until the following spring, when they were hired by the Department of Fisheries and Oceans to experiment for halibut along the Labrador coast. After the contract was completed, the *Vair* returned to North Sydney to prepare for her first season in the sword-fishery.

Fishing for sword aboard the *Vair* was a great success. On November 6, 1967, Captain Currie and his crew arrived at North Sydney, after a fourteen day trip. They had on board at the time, one of the largest catches ever landed by a longliner. They unloaded 75,075 pounds which broke the previous record in Canada of 63,000 pounds.

The success for the *Vair* and her crew continued, and three years later, they broke their own record, when they arrived in North Sydney with 80,240 pounds of swordfish in a sixteen-day trip.

Although very successful, the crew of the *Vair* had battered many storms, and there were times when they had barely escaped danger. A trip in the fall of 1970 would be one such voyage.

On September 25, 1970, the *Vair* departed North Sydney for a normal two-week trip to the swordfishing grounds in the vicinity of Sable Island. Her crew for the voyage were:

Maxwell Currie, captain, Port aux Basques
Gilbert Riles, mate, Port aux Basques
John Hann, engineer, Isle aux Morts
Cecil Hardy, Rose Blanche
Roy Butt, Harbour La Cou
Henry Ashward, Rose Blanche
Clifford Dingwell, Port aux Basques
Cornelius Harvey, Isle aux Morts

In the late afternoon of October 7, the crew had finished setting their forty-five miles of floating trawl for the next morning, and rested down below for the night. As the evening progressed, the winds had begun to increase from an early fall gale, and throughout the night and next morning, the winds were gusting to storm force.

The wind had caused havoc on the fishing grounds for the swordfishing fleet, simply because their trawl was floating trawl, and the high winds carried them miles from their original location. However, by dawn the next morning, Captain Currie had readied the *Vair* and her crew to retrieve the lengthy trawl.

Moments after Currie had gotten the *Vair* under way, a huge wave struck the longliner, and the railing on the afterdeck was damaged. The crew had to latch onto whatever they could find, trying to prevent themselves from being tossed around. Little did they know that their hardships for the day were not over.

Finally, at 14:00, the forty-five miles of trawl was back on board, and now Captain Currie was preparing for the next set. However, because they had drifted so far, it would take the captain several hours to get back to the location where they would normally commence setting the trawl.

By now the wind had diminished to gale force, and Captain Currie got the *Vair* under way back to the fishing grounds were they had been the previous day. Although the *Vair* was heavily powered, and had a normal sea speed some twelve knots, the speed was reduced somewhat because of the wind.

At 17:00, Currie blew the whistle for the crew to standby to commence setting the trawl. As the crew waited to start their duties, the *Vair* was hit by another huge wave which flooded the slaughter-house and then the afterdeck. Captain Currie reduced the speed instantly to see if everything was alright. He was immediately met by crew member Gilbert Riles who informed him that John Hann had been washed overboard while preparing a tub of swordfish hooks for the upcoming set. The water which flooded the slaughterhouse had exited through the doors and ran aft on the afterdeck. All of the crew had managed to find something to grab onto with the exception of John Hann.

At once, Captain Currie returned to the wheelhouse and turned the *Vair* around in the howling winds and sea in the hope of locating John Hann. Fortunately, as soon as he had the vessel heading down-wind, he had managed to catch a glimpse him.

The crew knew that time was limited for John Hann, and Gilbert Riles knew that the only way of saving him was to jump over the side after him. He also knew that someone would have to stay on board the longliner and skillfully manoeuvre the longliner close to Hann. With this in mind, Gilbert informed Currie that he would jump in the water with the rope, and that the captain would stay on board and bring the longliner as close as possible to the scene.

By this time, the *Vair* was downwind of Hann, so Captain Currie turned the vessel around again and made the second attempt running downwind, and in doing so, he noticed the hood of the rubber jacket that John Hann was wearing.

At the moment he was sighted, and close enough to reach, Gilbert Riles jumped from the deck of the *Vair* into the raging water.

At the very instant he had jumped, the *Vair* was hit by another wave, increasing the height Gilbert jumped. Fortunately however, when he landed, he was close enough to John Hann that he grabbed onto him. The two were hauled back alongside the longliner where John was taken aboard and then Gilbert. The crew conducted CPR on Hann who was unresponsive at the time.

After several attempts, John Hann was revived, and taken to the galley. The fishing trip was aborted and the captain set course for North Sydney at once. When they arrived, John Hann was taken to the hospital, were he received further medical care. From North Sydney, John returned home, and several days later, he joyfully attended his daughter's wedding.

Although the swordfishing industry was booming and the crew of the *Vair* very successful, the industry was somewhat short-lived. In the early 1970s, researchers found traces of mercury in the stock of the east coast, and from then on, sales dropped, making the voyages unprofitable.

The MV *Vair* arriving in Cape Broyle on February 11, 1990, loaded with cod and halibut after a trip to the Grand Banks while under the command of Captain Blackie Ross. (Photo courtesy of Blackie Ross).

With the swordfishery on the decline, Captain Currie turned over command of the *Vair* to Captain Thomas Chislett of North Sydney. In the meantime, Currie had taken command of the herring seiner MV *Pacific Venture.*

Unfortunately, the herring fishery was coming to an end on the south coast, and Captain Currie resumed command of the *Nancy N* for a short while engaged in the greysole fishery.

Then in fall of 1971, Captain Currie took a slight career change when he purchased his own vessel, a 46-foot longliner named the MV *Robbie & Brad.* Currie fished the *Robbie & Brad* for two years and sold her in 1973 when he took command of a herring carrier in Placentia Bay, named the MV *Jocelyn Charmaine.* Unfortunately, the herring fishery in this area declined as well.

The *Jocelyn Charmaine* was the last of the larger commands for Captain Currie. From then on, he remained in the inshore fishery and began boat building until he retired.

Despite the storms that John Hann had battered in his career, and the harrowing experience aboard the *Vair,* he still remained in the fishery aboard longliners until he retired. He passed away on January 17, 2001, at the age of seventy.

Gilbert Riles also remained in the longline fishery until it closed, and from there, he went to work on trawlers. After the trawler fishery declined, he changed his career at sea and joined commercial ship-

The MV *Jocelyn Charmaine* at Port Greville, NS. (Photo courtesy of the Wagstaff Collection, Age of Sail Heritage Centre, Port Greville NS).

ping industry, working on canadian coast guard ships where he still works today.

As for the *Vair*, she was later sold to a firm in Newfoundland where her wheelhouse was altered and she was coated with fiberglass. As of today, She still remains under her Newfoundland owners.

The Life and Times of Maxwell Purchase

In June 1987, I was just a young school boy growing up in La Poile, on the southwest coast of Newfoundland. The date June 20, was a day students longed for—school was over for the summer.

Summer holidays would be different for me that year. My father, Clarence Vautier Sr., and his crew, were fishing for the summer along the shores off Cape Breton in his 42-foot longliner, the MV *Fr. G. Morning Star*. Once school was out, I called my father and asked if I would be able to come and spend some time fishing with him. His response was yes, but that I must not come alone. To my dismay, I knew of no one travelling in that general direction.

The next day however, my luck changed for the better when the crew of another longliner from La Poile named the MV *Triple C* arrived home for a short break. The vessel was owned and operated by Maxwell "Max" Purchase and was fishing from the same area as my father. Immediately, I asked Max if I could travel back with him to meet my father. He objected in the beginning, but eventually he relented.

I knew that voyaging with Max would be no problem. Max Purchase was no stranger to travelling, and most certainly, no stranger to the shores of Cape Breton.

Maxwell Purchase was born in La Poile on July 26, 1953, the second youngest of nine children to William and Agnes Purchase. Max unfortunately, like his siblings, was faced with tragedy at a young age when their father became ill and passed away on July 5, 1955, at the age of forty-five. Max was not quite two-years old at the time.

Agnes Purchase who was just thirty-four at the time of her husband's death, was left to raise nine children on her own. Her youngest daughter Duclie, was born one month after William's death.

Although times were tough, Agnes Purchase strived and raised the nine children on her own. The children however, immediately began helping in any way they could.

Six of the nine children were boys, and they went to work as soon as they were old enough, thus providing for their mother to the best of their abilities. Max being the younger of the boys, followed his father's and brother's footsteps and became a fisherman.

In the spring of 1972, Max's older brother Russell had worked and fished several previous years in Cape Breton. Before returning to Cape Breton, Russell sent a telegram to Captain Murray Bungay in the hope of securing a berth for the upcoming year. Captain Bungay was a well-known captain and ran a 56-foot longliner named the MV *Jane Marie*. Captain Bungay replied and told Russell he would have a berth for him as soon as he was ready and as well as for anyone else he knew. Russell asked his brother Max if he wanted to go and Max agreed. In no time, the two brothers were en route to North Sydney to join the *Jane Marie*.

In late April, the *Jane Marie* was ready to go and departed North Sydney for the fishing grounds near Glace Bay. However, due to heavy ice in the Cabot Strait, the *Jane Marie* and several other long-liners such as the MV *Dougie J* had to be escorted out by an ice break-er. Finally, they cleared the ice and Captain Murray Bungay set course for the fishing grounds off the Cape Breton coast. At this time of the year, the *Jane Marie* was equipped with a "Danish Seine" which was used for catching greysole

On May 1, 1972, the *Jane Marie* and her three-man crew, Max, Russell, and Captain Bungay carried out a normal day's fishing some twelve miles from Glace Bay.

Shortly before noon, the net was set out. However, shortly after

The MV *Jane Marie* in North Sydney Harbour in 1956.
(Photo courtesy Ambrose McNeil).

having the net in the water, Captain Bungay noticed a difference in the vessel's stability. Immediately, he checked the engineroom, and soon discovered that the *Jane Marie* had sprung a leak and was taking on water at an alarming rate. Bungay turned on all the pumps immediately, but they could not slow down the ingress of water. Moments later, Captain Bungay sent out a distress call and ordered his crew to standby for the possibility of abandoning the vessel.

The crew of the *Jane Marie* were in luck. Not far from their vessel was MV *Elaine Judith*, who was fishing for greysole in the area and under the command of Murray's brother, Captain George Bungay.

Captain George Bungay heard the distress call, and at once, proceeded to rescue the distressed crew. After the crew was taken safely aboard the *Elaine Judith*, a towline was secured to the waterlogged *Jane Marie* with the hope of towing her back to port.

Unfortunately, the large amount of water had caused the *Jane Marie* to sink by the bow, thus making it difficult to tow the vessel. As

The MV *Jane Marie* sinking slowly by the bow while being towed by the MV *Elaine & Judith* on May 1, 1972. (Photo courtesy of Marilyn Purchase).

The MV *Jane Marie* being towed by the stern shortly before she sank on May 1, 1972. (Photo courtesy of Marilyn Purchase).

a result, the towline broke. Then the crew secured the towline to the stern of the *Jane Marie*, but the vessel was already too deep in the water. Eventually, the tow effort was abandoned and the distressed crew members were landed safely in North Sydney.

The ordeal never kept the fishermen from the water for long. In no time, they were back on the fishing grounds again, this time aboard the 57-foot longliner MV *Ellen & Robey*, where they fished for the remainder of the year. Late that fall, after the fishing along the shore of Cape Breton was over, Max and Russell returned home.

The next year, Max didn't return to Nova Scotia because he secured a berth aboard the longliner MV *Fr. G. Morning Star* with Captain Clarence Vautier Sr. of La Poile. Now Max would be able to spend more time home, and on July 18, 1973, he married his long-time sweetheart, seventeen-year-old Marilyn Organ also of La Poile. They subsequently settled down in La Poile to start a family.

For the next two years, things went well for the young couple, and on Christmas Eve of 1974, their first child was born. The newborn was named Christian Murray Purchase (after Captain Murray Bungay).

The proud parents arrived home in La Poile on January 3, 1975, but shortly after, the child became ill. Just three days after arriving home on January 6, 1975, baby Murray had to be taken to Channel Hospital and then later to hospital in Corner Brook.

In Corner Brook, the child's health did not improve, and he was then transferred to the Janeway Hospital for Sick Children in St. John's. Regretfully, his condition never improved and he

Maxwell Purchase on deck of the MV *Ella & Robey* in 1972 at North Sydney.
(Photo courtesy of Marilyn Purchase).

passed away at on February 15, 1975. His body was then brought to La Poile and laid to rest. Although the loss of their child was tragic, the young parents found the strength to continue on. Max remained in La Poile fishing aboard the *Fr. G. Morning Star* for the next couple of years.

In the spring of 1976, the *Fr. G. Morning Star* was engaged in the seal hunt. The seals were plentiful, but this would be Max's last year aboard the longliner. Earlier that summer, Max decided to change his career and went to join the trawler fleet owned by Penny & Sons in Ramea.

Seal hunting aboard the MV *Fr. G Morning Star* on Rose Blanche Bank in March 1976. (L-R) John Purchase, Maxwell Purchase, Ralph Organ, and Captain Clarence Vautier Sr. (Author's Collection).

The new trawler fleet was booming and the future look bright for the fishery. For Max and Marilyn, things looked good as well, for on June 3, 1976, Marilyn gave birth to a baby girl named Trina.

Although the baby looked healthy, shortly after her birth, she too became ill. Trina like her brother Murray, was also sent to the Janeway hospital in St. John's. To her parent's shock, her health did not improve either. That summer, in late August, doctors at the Janeway decided to send baby Trina, along with her parents, to Maryland in the United States.

An air-ambulance was sent to St. John's, to pick up the child and her parents, but at the time, Max was at sea aboard one of the trawlers. Marilyn got into contact with the owners, and they in turn, contacted the captain of the trawler who agreed to take Max to the nearest port which incidentally was Ramea. Shortly after arriving in Ramea, Max boarded the ferry for La Poile where he arrived later that day. From La Poile, he boarded a helicopter which took him and Marilyn to St. John's.

Unfortunately, as in many cases, time is always of the essence. Shortly after Max and Marilyn arrived in St. John's on August 26, 1976, Trina Purchase died before there was a chance to fly the child and her parents to Maryland. The body of baby Trina was taken back to La Poile and buried next to her brother Murray.

One could probably never imagine the grief these two young parents suffered after losing two children. However, through strength and courage, Max and Marilyn found the will to go on with their lives. Max returned to the trawlers and later worked his way up to mate and captain. Unfortunately, shortly after in 1983, the plant was hampered by strikes and lockouts. The next year, the Penny firm and its fleet of trawlers were sold to Fishery Products International.

With the strike in effect, the trawlers were tied to the dock and the crews were out of work. Shortly after, Max went to Port aux Basques and took command of the MV *Sand Lance*, a 65-foot stern trawler owned by T. J Hardy Limited.

Max continued to command the *Sand Lance* until the next year. In the winter of 1985, the inshore fishery was on an upturn, so Max

The MV *Pennyrowe* docked at the fish plant in Ramea.
(Photo courtesy of Jack Keeping).

The MV *Sea Shuttle* arriving in La Poile on February 27, 1990 heavy iced up.
(Photo courtesy of Valda Vautier).

decided to buy his own boat, a 35-foot longliner name the MV *Triple C*.

The hook and line fishery boomed for several years, and in 1989, it collapsed which resulted in many fishermen facing tough times. Max tried to avoid the downturn and returned to Cape Breton to fish aboard longliners once again. This time he boarded the MV *White Cap III*. His career was short aboard this vessel as well, as by this time, the longliner fleet in Cape Breton was being affected by catch rates and quotas.

In the winter of 1990, Max went back into the trawler fleet and went to Fortune to join his cousin Captain Archibald Bond, who was in command of the MV *Sea Shuttle*, a new 65-foot steel stern trawler. Unfortunately, Max's career aboard the *Sea Shuttle* was short, much like the *Sea Shuttle* herself. On Friday April 13, 1990, Captain Bond and his crew aboard the *Sea Shuttle* were fishing some 200 nautical

The MV *Sea Shuttle* berthed at St. John's, in March 1990.
(Photo courtesy of Valda Vautier).

miles off the Northeast coast of Newfoundland. Late that night, while returning to port, the vessel began to take on water. With more water than the pumps could keep up with, Captain Bond sent a mayday and abandoned the sinking trawler. They were later rescued by a coast guard ship and brought to St. John's.

Although none of the crew were strangers to being shipwrecked, it never kept them from fishing. After the sinking of the *Sea Shuttle*, Captain Bond took command of the MV *Straits Pride II*, a 65-foot trawler wooden stern trawler built in Trinity Bay, Newfoundland in 1982/1983.

Captain Bond fished the *Straits Pride II* for the summer and fall along the south and southwest coast, and in December, he moved east, fishing from the port of St. John's.

In the early morning of December 15, 1990, Captain Bond and the crew of the *Straits Pride II* departed St. John's for the fishing grounds known as Tobin's Point, a sixteen-hour journey in a north-easterly direction.

For the next couple of days, the catches were good, and in the early morning hours of December 17, 1990, the deck was secured and Captain Bond set course for the port of St. John's. The weather at the time consisted of southeast winds, a light swell, and drizzle.

But by mid-afternoon, the winds had increased to gale force, and the seas were gradually building. Not long after, the *Strait Pride II* and her crew were standing into danger when the chain on the port stabi-lizer broke, causing the vessel to list to starboard. Because of the heavy seas, it was decided that it would be too dangerous to raise the starboard stabilizer. Instead the port fuel tank was shut off, leaving the fuel consumption coming from the starboard tank only. They hoped this would help correct the starboard list.

Unfortunately, the list could not be corrected. As he called the coast guard, giving them the situation and requesting an escort, Captain Bond ordered the crew to don their lifejackets. The coast guard informed Captain Bond that the CCGS *Sir Wilfred Grenfell* would be dispatched in minutes.

At 16:04, Captain Bond contacted the coast guard again inform-

ing them that they would have to
abandon their vessel, and at this
time they were some forty miles
northeast of St. John's. By now, the
starboard railing was submerging,
making abandonment difficult. Still
the crew managed to launch the 18-
foot aluminum lifeboat and an inflat-

The MV *Straits Pride II.*

able liferaft. Three of the crew: Ross King, Robbie MacDonald, and
Harold Martin managed to make it into the liferaft.

Captain Archie Bond, Max Purchase, and Russell Bond were left
to cling to the lifeboat in the freezing waters of the North Atlantic.
Moments later, the *Straits Pride II* rolled over and sank stern first.
Shortly after, the liferaft drifted away, and that was the last time
Archie, Russell, and Max were seen alive.

At 23:30, the three crew members in the liferaft heard an aircraft
and consequently fired flares in the hope of attracting attention. The
flares were seen by the aircraft and reported to the CCGS *Sir Wilfred
Grenfell.* They fired several more flares later that night when they first
sighted the lights of the coast guard ship.

The search for Archie, Russell, and Max continued throughout
the night, and by 10:00 on December 18, one of the bodies were
found. Not long after, the remaining two bodies were also recovered
and all of them were taken to St. John's. Archie Bond (aged thirty-
one) left a common-law wife, a daughter, and a son who was born
shortly after his father death; Russell (aged forty-three), brother of the
Archie left a wife and three sons; and Max (aged thirty-seven) left his
wife.

Several days later, the bodies of all three fishermen were taken to
their homes and laid to rest.

Fire On Board the
Wanda R. Deborah

Preserving the maritime history along the south and southwest coast would have not been possible without the help of several people from a number of communities. One such person who aided tremendously is Walter S. Bond, a fisherman from Burnt Islands, Newfoundland.

Walter S. Bond was born in La Poile, the son of Archibald and Hazel Bond, who when Walter was a child, resettled from La Poile to the community of Burnt Islands. Like many young Newfoundlanders, Walter left home and went to work in the fish plant at Trepassey in 1959. After working the summer and early fall, he returned home and then turned his career to the sea, signing on board an 82-foot coaster name the MV *Zahm* in December 1959. The next year, Walter returned to the sea again, this time in a bigger ship and travelled further away from home. The vessel was a 150-foot coaster name the MV *Mayfal*.

The *Mayfal* was under command of another Burnt Islands native named Captain Thomas Edmunds. While on board the *Mayfal*, Walter and his shipmates would load fish in Newfoundland and carry the load to the West Indies. The return trip consisted of cargo such as rum, salt, and molasses.

After a short stint in the coasting trade, Walter remained at sea, but turned to fish on board longliners. At the time, otter trawlers were on the rise, resulting in Walter going to work on them. His first trip was on the 85-foot *Zibet*, under command of another well-known captain named James Chaulk, who was also from Burnt Islands. After several years under the command of Captain Chaulk, and learning the necessary skill, Walter then commanded trawlers such as the MV *Senator Penny*, MV *Cape Keltie*, and the MV *Acadia Crest*.

In 1973, after ten years in the trawler industry, Captain Walter Bond decided to try a different approach and buy his own boat. He purchased a 55-foot wooden fishing boat name the MV *Lady Philpott* and later he renamed her the MV *Wanda R. Deborah*, after his three children.

In the spring of 1975, Walter and his crew, Roland Keeping and Walter's brother Russell were fishing for american plaice (known locally as greysole) off the east coast of Cape Breton near Ingonish.

American Plaice was normally caught between dusk and dawn, which meant that after the last tow, the vessel would return to port. In the early morning hours of June 27, 1975, the *Wanda R. Deborah* departed the little fishing community of New Haven, Cape Breton Island, for the fishing grounds, just over an hour away.

When the crew arrived on the fishing grounds, the buoy was dropped, and the first half of the long rope-like warp was set out, and then the net. Once the net was out, the crew began to set out the second half.

Just before the second half of the warp was out, and they were about to pick up the buoy, Captain Bond, who was in the wheelhouse, saw smoke rising from the engineroom through a vent, which supplied outside air to the engineroom. Bond immediately went to investigate further. He raised the engineroom hatch to see where the smoke was coming from, but the instant he lifted the hatch, a explosion occurred. The blast rocked the whole vessel and flames were everywhere. The fire erupted in the amidships area and Captain Bond was now trapped in the wheelhouse.

The *Wanda R. Deborah* was equipped with a deck engine, and the fuel tank was located exactly where the fire had erupted. Captain Bond knew that it would be too dangerous to combat the fire as the fuel tank for the deck engine could explode any minute.

Consequently, he ordered the remaining two crew members to lower the dory which was unfortunately located on the roof above the fire.

They managed to get the dory down on the main deck, but in the process of lowering it, they dropped it over the side, capsizing it. Meanwhile, Captain Bond who was still in the wheelhouse, knew he had to get past the fire and abandon the burning vessel. As a result, he decided to make a brave dash through the inferno. He did just that, but suffered severe burns.

Now all three crew members were on the main deck with no lifeboat. They only had other one alternative, to jump overboard. Moments later, they plunged over the side abandoning the *Wanda R. Deborah*.

The crew were unfortunate in many ways, however, they were fortunate in others. Fishing not far from the *Wanda R. Deborah* was the MV *Claude & Roy* from New Haven, Nova Scotia. The vessel immediately came to the aid of the distressed fishermen and they were pulled from the water shortly after jumping. Walter, of course, who had suffered severe burns, was in the worst condition. He was hastily taken to the nearest hospital which was Neil's Harbour. He arrived there that afternoon.

Walter went straight to the operating room where doctors spent three and half hours attaching skin graphs to his burns. The recovery process was slow and he remained in hospital for another six weeks.

The fate of the *Wanda R. Deborah* was exactly what Captain Bond had thought. She was rocked by another explosion and was blown in half and sank. Although it was a horrifying experience, the crew remained fishing; Russell later lost his life at sea. Walter remained in command for years after. When the fishery closed, Walter returned to commercial shipping. Roland remained in the fishery, but on the processing side in the local fish plant.

The Wreck of the Lady Maria

The waters of St. Pierre Bank and the Grand Banks along the south and east coast of Newfoundland have been prosperous and lucrative fishing grounds to fishermen from Canada and various other countries. These waters are famous due to the wide variety and vast abundances of species Another factor which made these fishing grounds so famous was its size, as they cover hundreds of miles of ocean floor.

St. Pierre Bank is the smaller of the two, running almost parallel along the south coast of Newfoundland. Its depth gradually increases to the southward and southwestward until it meets the eastern side of the Laurentian Channel, where the depth suddenly drops to hundreds of metres. The Laurentian Channel runs all the way from the Atlantic Ocean to the Cabot Strait, finally ending at the St. Lawrence River.

In late spring and early summer, the water temperature in these waters are still relatively cold compared to the warm air flowing up from the south. When the warm water flows over the cooler water, a weather phenomenon known as fog occurs. As a result, from late spring until early summer, twenty to thirty percent of the days are hampered with poor visibility of less than half a mile.

Due to the fact that these fishing grounds cover such a large area, commercial ships constantly navigate these very waters, especially when foreign vessels depart ports in Europe and the Far East destined for ports in Nova Scotia and Quebec. With poor visibility and such a high volume of vessel traffic, mishaps in such a area would seem inevitable. Consequently, this was just the case for two vessels in the late spring of 1978.

Shortly before noon on June 12, 1978, the 115-foot stern trawler MV *Lady Maria* slipped her lines from her berth in Alder Point, Cape Breton Island, for a routine fishing trip to the Grand Banks, some 200 miles away. The vessel was owned by United Maritime Limited of New Brunswick and carried a crew of thirteen. Eleven of the known crew are listed below:

Frederick Davies, captain
Joseph Savoury Jr., mate
Gerald Savoury, seaman
Roland Savoury, seaman
James Seymour, seaman
Gary Edmunds, seaman

Robert Worthington, seaman
Mike Pero, engineer
Dawson Walker, cook
William "Billy" Ward
James Fraser, seaman

Late on the evening of June 12, 1978, the *Lady Maria* was passing some fifty miles south of St. Pierre, over the southern part of St. Pierre Bank. The weather conditions consisted of thick fog and light winds, along with a heavy swell.

The normal watch procedure for the bridge was set up for two

The MV *Lady Maria* during refit in Georgetown, PEI, in 1971.
(Photo courtesy of Fred Davidson).

crew members per watch at one time, with two hours on and four hours off. At 20:00, crew members Gary Edmunds and James Seymour began their watch. The visibility remained nearly zero due to the fog, so both crew members constantly monitored the radars and placed close vigilance on another ship in the area they detected on radar.

At 21:30, crew member Gary Edmunds awoke the next watch which consisted of shipmates Roland Savoury and James Fraser, who would start work at 22:00.

After a quick coffee and light lunch, Roland Savoury and James Fraser arrived on the bridge at 22:00 and took over the shift. They were informed by the previous watch of another ship in the area that they were watching closely. However, due to the cutter caused by the heavy swell, it was difficult to determine where the target was.

The speed of the *Lady Maria* was reduced to a near stop to give the crew more time to assess the situation and in the hope of avoiding a collision. Unfortunately, the events did not unfold as they had hoped. At 22:20, the bow of the other ship, which turned out to be the 15,000-ton bulk carrier MV *Marka L* (en route to St. Lawrence River Port from Europe) struck the starboard quarter of the *Lady Maria* with a devastating impact.

The MV *Marka L* shown here upbound the St. Lawrence River on May 17, 1993. (Photo by René Beauchamp).

Roland knew by the impact that the *Lady Maria* had suffered considerable damage, but did not know exactly how much. He then ran to the galley/accommodation area and shouted to the rest of the crew informing them of what had happened. The crew on the other hand had already awakened from the noise of the collision.

Moments after the impact, the *Lady Maria* slowly began to take on water, but in amounts more than her pumps could handle. The bulkheads between the engineroom and the fish hold were busted, and the dory which was secured in the cradle on deck, was demolished as well. The *Marka L*, on the other hand, received several holes in her bulbous bows, but it was easily emptied out by the vessel's large pumps.

The bow and the wheelhouse of the *Lady Maria* was located forward, and being the highest part of the trawler, gave the crew the only hope of being rescued. The captain of the *Marka L* then noticed that all of the distressed crew members had gathered on the trawler's bow, so he backed away from the starboard quarter and placed the bow of his ship near the bow of the *Lady Maria*. They then lowered two rope ladders over the bow of his ship and down unto the bow of the *Lady Maria* allowing the crew to escape.

Captain Davidson was still at the helm of the *Lady Maria*, and because the engine was still running, he was able to keep the bow of the trawler tight to the bow of the *Marka L* so the men could easily climb the ladder one at a time. Including the captain, there were nine crew members to climb the two ladders: Roland Savoury, Gerald Savoury, William Ward, and Robert Worthington had already launched a rubber liferaft and were floating nearby the sinking trawler.

However, there were still two crew members on board the *Lady Maria*; Captain Davidson and the mate, Joseph Savoury Jr. Now that there were only two left, the captain was going to grab one ladder and for Joseph Savoury Jr. to grab the other. Because the swell was high, and the bow of the *Lady Maria* rose and fell against the bow of the *Marka L*, Captain Davidson informed Joseph and the remainder of the crew to only board the ladder when the sinking trawler was going down on the swell. That way they would not get knocked off by the weight of the trawler.

Davidson jumped for the ladder and informed Savoury to do the same. Unfortunately, the very scenario that Captain Davidson tried to avoid happened. Mere moments after Joseph Savoury Jr. stepped on the ladder, the bow of the two vessels crashed together and he was

Charles Savoury, Joseph Savoury Jr., and David Savoury at Rose Blanche in 1976. (Photo courtesy of Margaret Savoury).

knocked off the ladder and into the water. More than likely, he was killed instantly and because of the thick fog and heavy seas, the body of the young fisherman was never found.

The captain of the *Marka L* then backed the vessel away from the bow of the *Lady Maria* and retrieved the liferaft and the four crew members. They then resumed the search for the body of Joseph Savoury Jr. along with the help from another bulk carrier the MV *Lynton Grange*. Later the search was aided by a fisheries patrol vessel MV *Nonia*, but all that was found was a oil slick and some debris.

Early on the morning of June 13, after several hours of searching, the *Marka L* departed the seen of the collision and headed for the port of St. John's. She docked at the finger pier at 20:30 on June 13 under escort of the *Nonia*. Meanwhile, the Canadian Destroyer *Skeena* remained in the area after all other vessels had left the area, but the fog had reduced the visibility to nil and hampered their search efforts.

Several days after the accident, the search for Joseph Savoury Jr. was called off. At the time of death he was twenty-eight years old and married with two children. The remainder of the crew stayed in St John's for several days then returned to their respective homes.

Tragedy in La Poile

The morning of April 20, 1982, started out as a typical day for the residents of La Poile, a small outport community located on the southwest coast of Newfoundland, some thirty-three miles east of Port aux Basques. La Poile, like many Newfoundland communities, depended mainly on the fishery, which included lobsters and salmon in the spring and cod for the remainder of the year.

During the spring of 1982, cod catches were good along the southwest coast, and although it was the beginning of the lobster season, all of the fishermen were fishing for cod. As for the salmon season, it would not be open until May 15. Apart from several small longliners, the majority of the fishermen fished individually in open boats powered by outboard motors.

At 09:00, local fisherman Clarence Vautier Sr. had just departed La Poile in his 42-foot longliner, the MV *Fr. G Morning Star*. The longliner and her crew were under charter to T. J. Hardy Limited of Port aux Basques to collect fish in La Poile and Grand Bruit. From there, their job was to bring it to the processing plant at Rose Blanche. Making up the crew of the *Fr. G Morning Star*, along with Captain Vautier Sr., was his twenty-year-old son Raymond, twenty-year-old Dave Neil, and twenty-one-year-old Wayne Francis, all of La Poile.

As the day went by, things were normal. Fishermen were gradually returning from the fishing grounds, the coastal ferry MV *Petite Forte* had made a brief stop at La Poile on her routine trip from Port aux Basques to Terrenceville; the women were carrying out their daily chores, and the children were attending school. One of the fishermen from La Poile who was on the fishing grounds that morning was forty-

Henry Neil at his home in La Poile in 1961.
(Photo courtesy of Evelyn Neil).

six-year-old Henry Neil. Henry was fishing alone in his 19-foot open boat that was powered by a twenty-horsepower outboard motor.

Henry, like the rest of the fishermen, had left home early that morning to set his trawl along the west side of La Poile Bay, in an area known "Out Long Shore." Once he had the trawl set out in this area, he proceeded to the east side of the bay to retrieve the trawl he had set the previous night.

Like many pervious mornings, the catches were good, and at 08:30, Henry arrived at the local fish wharf in La Poile were he unloaded his catch of nearly a 1,000 pounds of cod to weigh master Melvin Bond.

Once the fish was unloaded, Henry moored his boat at his own wharf and was met by Brian Chant, his future son-in-law. Brian helped Henry to off-load his trawl, and once it was done, Brian began to re bait the trawl while Henry went home to grab a quick lunch. Brian was a deckhand aboard the 115-foot side trawler MV *Penny Luck II* at the time and would have normally been at sea. However, due to mechanical trouble, the trawler was delayed .

At 10:00, Henry finished his lunch and departed La Poile to retrieve the trawl he had set that morning. He informed his wife Evelyn that he should be back home around 14:00 if all went well. The fishing grounds were located just several miles from La Poile Harbour.

However, when 14:00 came around, Henry had not returned home and his wife Evelyn became concerned. Evelyn then asked her eighteen-year-old daughter Cathy if she would ask Brian to go and

Henry and son David at a wedding reception in La Poile, August 1980.
(Photo courtesy of Evelyn Neil).

look for him. Brian, by this time, had finished baiting Henry's trawl, and had just started baiting some trawl for his nephew Ross Francis. However, as soon as Cathy mentioned Henry's delay, Brian departed La Poile immediately.

Upon his arrival on the fishing grounds, Brian didn't see anything at first, but a short while later, he noticed a small boat sitting low in the water, approximately half-a-mile from the shoreline. He headed his boat for the location at once and soon discovered that the boat was Henry's. The boat was completely swamped with some of the trawl missing. The tools for the outboard motor, which Henry normally carried in a five gallon bucket was dumped. Only the empty pail remained at the bottom of the boat. However, there was no sign of Henry.

Brian searched the boat high and low, but saw no sign of Henry. He then decided to return to the shoreline hoping that Henry may have gotten ashore in a nearby cove. However, his search revealed nothing.

Brian then decided to return to the location of Henry's swamped boat for another look. After searching around the boat more closely this time, Brian noticed something peculiar floating in the water some 300 yards past the location of the boat. He soon discovered that what he saw was the body of Henry Neil. The only thing keeping him afloat was a small air pocket in his jacket.

With all his might, Brian pulled Henry's body aboard. The only thing missing on him were his boots and dentures. Once Brian had him on board, he rolled his body over and gave him give mouth to mouth resuscitation. After several minutes, he realized he could not revive him.

At 15:30, family and residents saw Brian entering the harbour waving his hands to attract attention. Upon seeing this, everyone knew then something must have gone wrong. When he arrived at the wharf below Henry's house, family and residents were in shock, for lying across the thwart of Brian's boat, was the body of the young fisherman. Henry's body was taken ashore, and later that evening, carried to Rose Blanche by the longliner MV *Edna & Deborah*.

By now, the *Fr. G. Morning Star* had arrived at Rose Blanche, off-loaded her cargo of fish, and was preparing to depart again for the trip back home. As mentioned earlier, Dave Neil was a member of the crew and also the son of Henry Neil. Shortly before they were ready to depart, the manager of the fish plant, Frederick Billard, called Captain Vautier Sr. to the office. Mr. Billard informed the

Henry and granddaughter Kelly during Christmas 1981. (Photo courtesy of Evelyn Neil).

captain that he had just received a call from La Poile with some tragic news for crew member David Neil.

Captain Vautier Sr. immediately grew concerned because his daughter Sandra and Dave Neil had a six-month-old daughter Kelly. Instantly, Captain Vautier Sr. thought that something must have happened to the child.

Although the message was not of that nature, the news could not have been more tragic. Mr. Billard informed Vautier of the accident involving Dave's father. Captain Vautier Sr. then returned to the longliner and met Dave in galley where he passed him the horrible news. Shortly before 18:00, the *Fr. G. Morning Star* departed Rose Blanche and arrived in La Poile shortly after 19:00. Once here, Dave joined the rest of his family.

Although the circumstances leading up to the accident will never be known, one thing seems certain, Henry must have fought to keep the boat afloat. In defence of this, three tubs of the trawl were missing from the boat when Brian discovered it. Most likely, the trawl would have been in the bottom of the boat and therefore it would have been very difficult for it to have come out of the boat. This suggests that Henry must have dumped the trawl in the hope of not swamping the craft. Secondly, the tool bucket was dumped and there was no sign of engine trouble. Even if Henry did experience engine trouble, it is highly unlikely he would have dumped out all of the tools. It does seem likely that the tools were discarded so Henry could use the bucket as a bailer. Also, only a small amount of cod was left aboard the boat, so Henry may have decided to dump them as well.

As in most of the tragedies at sea, the exact cause will never be known. One only knows that on this particular day, the winds were light, and seas were calm. For Henry to retrieve his trawl and be on his way home, the accident could not have occurred long before Brian arrived. Also, the coastal ferry would have passed very close to the location where Henry was found on her normal route. If they had noticed anything out of the ordinary, they would have certainly reported it or offered assistence.

Two days after the accident, in the late afternoon of April 22, the body of Henry Neil was returned to La Poile by the longliner MV *Cape Anguille*, under the command of Edward Bernard of Rose Blanche. His body was waked in the La Poile church until the next day when he was laid to rest in the cemetery next to his mother. At the time, Henry left a wife Evelyn (aged thirty-eight), and five children:

Henry Neil with all his children (l-r) Cathy, Corina, David, Darrell, and Claudine during Christmas 1973. (Photo courtesy of Evelyn Neil).

Dave (aged twenty), Cathy (aged eighteen), Claudine (aged sixteen), Corina (aged fourteen), and Darrell (aged eight).

Although Henry had lost his life fishing, his son Dave still decided to follow in his father's footsteps. Dave's younger brother Darrell, also followed his father's career, and he too became a fisherman. Several years after his father's death, he relocated to Port aux Basques with his mother. Henry's oldest daughter Cathy, remained in La Poile and married Brian Chant the next year. His two younger daughters, Claudine and Corinna, moved out of La Poile later on to attend school. Claudine now resides in Brampton, Ontario, while Corinna lives in St. John's.

As for Henry's 19-foot speedboat, she was towed to La Poile later that day. A few days later, it was hauled ashore on the south side of La Poile Harbour, where she remained for years, until she was intentionally burned on a Guy Fawke's night.

Collision Off Cape Race

In the early 1960s, the fishing industry in Canada was experiencing some of its first new trawlers that were being built in shipyards in Canada and around the world. In Newfoundland, the large steel trawlers were destined for the ports with large fish plants such as Harbour Breton, Fortune, Burgeo, Ramea, and Burin. One of the larger firms was Booth Fisheries, who operated side trawlers out of Mulgrave, Nova Scotia, and Fortune, Newfoundland. In the later years, the trawlers of the Booth Fisheries fleet was managed by another company in Fortune known as The Lake Group.

One of the trawlers operated by The Lake Group was the MV *Barbara B. Fletcher*, a 125-foot side trawler built in Alphen A/D Riji, Holland, in 1960. Throughout her career, she was commanded by several different captains, but in the fall of 1981, she was placed under the command of Captain Mike Billard of Grand Bank, formerly of Grand Bruit. Captain Billard was no stranger to the sea or to trawlers. The first side trawler was the MV *Neptune VI* out of Burgeo, under Captain Ingram. After that he went to work on another side trawler named the MV *Burhound,* under Captain Walter Carter, also from Burgeo. Billard later went on to captain trawlers himself, taking his first command on the side trawler *Barbara B. Fletcher.*

Captain Billard's first trips in the *Barbara B. Fletcher* were successful, but as any seaman knows, success does not always come easily. In February of 1982, just several months after taking command of the *Barbara B. Fletcher,* Billard and his crew were fishing 100 miles south of Cape Race, in an area known as the Eastern Gully, when a winter storm raged over the whole east coast of Canada. The same storm claimed the oil platform *Ocean Ranger* and her eighty-four crew members.

Throughout the storm, Captain Billard managed to keep his trawler seaworthy, and eventually they weathered out the storm. The following day, Billard berthed the *Barbara B. Fletcher* at the port of Fermeuse, fully loaded with cod and flounder.

On May 3, 1982, the *Barbara B. Fletcher* was berthed at the dock in Fortune, fully restocked for another trip to the fishing grounds. Her crew for the upcoming trip were as follows:

Mike Billard, captain, Grand Bank
Robert Cox, mate, Grand Bank
Cecil Penny, chief engineer, Fortune
Jerry Ingram, second engineer, Fortune
Thomas Mavin, cook, Fortune
Robert MacDonald, bosun, Lord's Cove
Ralph Coffey, deckhand, Lord's Cove
Raymond Felix, deckhand, Fortune
Brian Remo, deckhand, Fortune
Leo Martin, deckhand, Fortune
Junior Brushett, deckhand, Fortune
John Stacey, deckhand, Point May
Edgar Hillier, deckhand, Point May

Shortly after breakfast on May 4, 1982, the vessel departed the port of Fortune for the fishing grounds on the northeast portion of the Grand Banks in an area known as "Woolfall Bank." The grounds were located some sixty miles east of Cape Race and roughly 250 miles from the port of Fortune. The journey to the fishing grounds would normally take between twenty-five and thirty hours.

Shortly before midnight on May 4, Captain Billard was relieved on the bridge by Mate Robert Cox. The weather consisted of light winds and sea, along with heavy fog. Billard then left the bridge and went to his room which was adjacent to the wheelhouse. Before settling down for the night, the captain unpacked his fishing clothes

MV *Barbara B. Fletcher* tied up at the fish plant in Grand Bank.
(Maritime History Archives, Captain Harry Stone Collection).

and laid them by his bunk for easy retrieval in the morning. On top
of his clothes he placed his knife, something that was always carried
by trawlermen.

In the early morning hours of May 5, 1982, the *Barbara B.
Fletcher* was navigating in dense fog about twelve miles east of Cape
Race. Not far ahead of the vessel was the side trawler MV *Zerda*,
under the command of Captain Thomas Lawrence from Harbour
Breton, who was also headed for the fishing grounds. Also steaming
in the area of the two trawlers was the 680-foot bulk carrier MV
Maritime Alliance, en route to Montreal from Europe.

At 03:30, while manoeuvring in the dense fog, the *Maritime
Alliance* and *Barbara B. Fletcher* collided. The bow of the *Maritime
Alliance* struck the portside of the *Barbara B. Fletcher*, just forward
of the wheelhouse, and then sheared towards her stern, creating
further damage along the portside.

When Captain Mike Billard felt the impact, he ran to the wheelhouse immediately. When he looked through the wheelhouse door, the stern section of the *Maritime Alliance* was just passing. He also knew that his vessel would be quickly taking on water.

Captain Billard instantly knew the urgency of the situation and issued a mayday. At the time of the collision, the majority of the crew were asleep. The impact against the portside created difficulty for the men to get out of their rooms because the doors were jammed by the bent metal. Fortunately however, everyone was able to get out of their cabins and muster on deck. They inflated the two liferafts and immediately abandoned the sinking trawler.

Captain Billard remained on board and made another call, this time to Captain Lawrence on the *Zerda*, telling him of the mishap. Captain Lawrence immediately turned his vessel around and headed for the distressed fishermen. After the call to Captain Lawrence, Captain Billard left the bridge to abandon the sinking trawler. At this time, the water was just entering the wheelhouse of the sinking trawler.

When Captain Billard arrived on deck, he was advised by his

The MV *Maritime Alliance* upbound the St. Lawrence River in May 1982.
(Photo by René Beauchamp).

shipmates that the two liferafts were still secured to the deck. Captain Billard reached for his knife, that he had taken out the night before, and cut the liferafts free. Just as he did so, the trawler sank beneath him, and he floated off of the deck and into the water. As he swam away from the sinking trawler, he looked over his shoulder. All that could be seen was a small portion of the bow remaining above the surface.

Not long after getting into the liferafts, Captain Billard and his crew were picked by the crew of the *Zerda*. From there they were taken to the port of Fermeuse were they arrived later that day.

Although the crew of the *Barbara B. Fletcher* had a narrow escape, it didn't keep them from going to sea. After the sinking of their vessel, Captain Billard took command of another side trawler named the MV *Thomas L. Garland*, and from there, he made several trips as mate on the stern trawler MV *Canso Condor*. He later took command again, on the stern trawler MV *Fortune Endeavour*, and

The MV *Grand Knight*. (Author's Collection).

then of a seiner for Fishery Products named the MV *Newfoundland Arrow*. After a few years aboard the seiner, Captain Billard returned to trawlers captaining the MV *Grand Knight* until he retired.

BIBLIOGRAPHY BY STORY

The Mystery of the Maud Gilliam

Anglican Church Records, PANL.
Mercantile Navy List, 1894.
The Evening Telegram, December 3, 1895

The Wreck of the Fiona

Anglican Church Records, PANL.
The Western Star, September 28, 1900.
The Western Star, October 16, 1900.
The Western Star, November 2, 1900.

Tragedy at East Bay

Conversation with Ernest Farrell, Cobourg, ON (Deceased).
Vital Statistics 1921.

The Wreck of the Donald L. Silver

Conversation with John L. Hackett, Terrenceville, NL.
Mercantile Navy List, 1923.
The Daily News, January 12, 1924.
The Humber Log, "Looking Back Into History," January 17, 1973.
Unidentified clipping.

Tragedy at Grand Bruit

Conversation with Clarence Billard, Corner Brook, NL.
St. John's Register of Shipping, 1927.

The Loss of the Hilda

Conversation with Carol Keeping, Burnt Islands, NL.
The Evening Telegram, April 11–12, 1927.
The Western Star, April 20, 1927.

The Loss of the Vianna

Anglican Church Records, PANL,
The Halifax Chronicle, August 27, 1927.

The Loss of Three Rose Blanche Fishermen

Anglican Church Records, PANL
Conversation with Annabella King, St. John's, NL.
Correspondence from Marion Robar, Rhodes Corner, Lunenburg Co., NS.
Mercantile Navy List 1928, 1931, and 1942.
The Halifax Chronicle, March 23, 1929.
Sydney Post-Record, March 29, 1929.
Sydney Post-Record, February 27, 1931.

West Point Tragedy

Conversation with Violet Taylor, Port aux Basques, NL.
The Western Star, May 4, 1932.

The Strickland Family Tragedies

Anglican Church Records, PANL.
Conversation with Annie Buckland, Harbour Le Cou, NL.
Mercantile Navy List, 1928.

The Loss of the Julia A. Anderson

Conversation with Athena Wagg Buckland, Harbour Le Cou, NL.
St. John's Registry of Shipping, 1936.
Sydney Post-Record, April 23, 1936.
The Daily News, April 16, 18, and 20, 1936.

The Wreck of the Mizpah

The Gulf News, November 21, 1984.

Medals of Bravery

Conversations with Reg Munden, Calgary, AB; Gordon Hardy, North
Ingonish, NS; and Nathan LeMoine, Rose Blanche, NL (now residing in
St. John's, NL).
Mercantile Navy List, 1936.
Sydney Post-Record, January 7, 1937 and June 29, 1939.
The Halifax Herald, October 24–25, 1940.

The Wreck of the Ruth Marie

Conversation with George Billard, Grand Bruit, NL.
Mercantile Navy List, 1942.

Dorymen From the Freda M

Conversation with Nathan LeMoine, Rose Blanche, NL (now residing in St. John's, NL).
Mercantile Navy List, 1944.
The Evening Telegram, "Offbeat History" by Michael Harrington, May 20, 1986.
Vital Statistics 1944, PANL.

The Adventures of Captain Thomas Chislett

Conversations with Dennis Chislett, Barrie, ON; Emery Stevens, Chester, NS; Nathan LeMoine, Rose Blanche, NL (now residing in St. John's, NL); and Gilbert Riles, Port aux Basques, NL.
Halifax Register of Shipping, 1956 and 1957.

The Life and Times of the Chislett Brothers

Conversations with Dan Chislett, Rose Blanche and Harriett Warren, Margaree, NL.
Registry of Shipping 1935, 1945, and 1964.
Sydney Post-Record, May 27th, 1944.

Crewman Lost From the Mary J. W. Calman

Conversation with Ruby Munden, Isle aux Morts, NL.
Register of Shipping, St. John's, NL, 1942.
Sydney Post-Record, October 9, 1946.
The Daily News, October 10, 1946.

Astray From the Margaret M. Riggs

Dories and Dorymen by Otto Kelland.
Mercantile Navy List ,1948.
Conversations with George Warren, Corner Brook, NL, and Harold Keeping, North Sydney, NS.

Lost From the Betty & Audrey

Conversation with John R. Hardy, Rose Blanche, NL.
Mercantile Navy List, 1935.
The Daily News, March 19, 1949.
The Western Star, March 20, 1949.

Mishap At Sea: The Captain James Buffett Story

Conversation with John R. Hardy, Rose Blanche, NL, and Dulcie Eavis, Florida, USA.
St. John's Register of Shipping, 1945.
The Post-Record, June 22, 1950.

Collision in Port aux Basques Harbour

Conversation with George Warren, Corner Brook, NL.
Mercantile Navy List, 1950.
St. John's Register of Shipping, 1939.

Crewman Lost From the Linda Diane

Conversation with John R. Hardy, Rose Blanche, NL; Marcella Kendall, Ramea, NL; and Harold Keeping, North Sydney, NS.

Cape Breton Post, November 26, 1956.
Halifax Register of Shipping, 1954
The Chronicle-Herald, August 28, 1959.

The Wreck of the Harry B. Nickerson III

Conversation with Edward Ingram, North Sydney, NS.
Correspondence from Doug Levy, Edmonton, AB.
List of Shipping, 1957.
Cape Breton Post, November 17, 1958.
Mercantile Navy List, 1940.

The Loss of Stanley Rose

Conversation with Gary Rose, St. John's, NL.
Confessions of a Boatbuilder by James D. Rosborough.
St. John's Register of Shipping, 1945.
The Western Star, December 2, 1963.

The Storm of 1964

Conversations with Harold Keeping, North Sydney, NS; Blackie Ross,
Cape Sable Island, NS; Walter Bond, Burnt Islands, NL; Isaac Hubert,
Havre-Aux-Maisons, QC; George Greene, Petit De Grat, NS; and Albert
Fanning, Little Dover, NS.
Correspondence with André Guévremont, Sorel, QC.
List of Shipping, 1964.
The Chronicle-Herald, December 2–5, 8–11, and 14, 1964.

Adrift Aboard the Carroll Brothers

Cape Breton Post, September 20, 1965.

Conversation with Alvin Carroll, Margaree, NL.
St. John's Register of Shipping, 1960

Blackout Aboard the Zarp

Conversation with Ephriam MacDonald, Burnt Islands, NL.
List of Shipping, 1966.
The Daily News, October 3, 1966.

The Wreck of the Zebra

Conversations with Walter Bond and Cynthia Harris, Burnt Islands, NL, and Alexander Lefrense, Isle aux Morts, NL.
List of Shipping, 1966.

Collision in Halifax Harbour

Conversations with Edwin Hardy Jr. Rose Blanche, NL, and Joseph Wilneff, Glace Bay, NS (Deceased).
Halifax Register of Shipping, 1957 and 1964.

Collision in the Cabot Strait

Cape Breton Post, April 28, 1969.
Conversation with Herman Guptill, Church Point, NS.
List of Shipping, 1969.

The Wreck of the Eastcliffe Hall

Conversation with Mark Durnford, Coldbrook, NS.
List of Shipping, 1970.

The Vair

Cape Breton Post, October 10, 1970.
Conversations with Maxwell Currie and Gilbert Riles, Port aux Basques, NL.
List of Shipping, 1967.

The Life and Times of Maxwell Purchase

Cape Breton Post, May 3, 1972.
Conversations with Marilyn Purchase; Raymond Vautier; Clarence Vautier
Sr., La Poile, NL; Russell Purchase, Catalina, NL; and Lew Munden, Port
aux Basques, NL.
List of Shipping, 1956.

Fire On Board the Wanda R. Deborah

Conversation with Walter Bond, Burnt Islands, NL.
List of Shipping, 1974.

The Wreck of the Lady Maria

Conversations with Gerald and Roland Savoury, Burnt Islands, NL, and
Fred Davidson, Glace Bay, NS.
List of Shipping, 1977.
The Evening Telegram, June 14–15, 1978.
The Western Star, June 13, 1978.

Tragedy in La Poile

Conversations with Evelyn Neil, Brian and Cathy Chant, David Neil, and
Clarence S. Vautier Sr., La Poile, NL.

Collision Off Cape Race

Conversation with Mike Billard, Grand Bank, NL.
List of Shipping, 1982.

INDEX

Neil, Kelly 195
Neil, William 16, 17
Neil's Harbour 43, 83, 184
MV *Nellie Cluett* 71
MV *Neptune* 198
New Brunswick 123, 138, 153, 154, 156, 186
New Chelsea 53–54, 159
MV *Newfoundland Arrow* 202
New Harbour 27, 51
New Haven 183–184
Newman, Clifford 156
Newport, George 69
MV *Nina W. Corkum* 71
MV *Nonia* 190
MV *Nora Harriett* 82
North Bay 6–8, 17, 42, 53, 83, 98–99, 132
North Sydney 1, 30–31, 43, 56, 58–65, 73–80, 83, 87–88, 93, 97–99, 101–102, 104–105, 107–113, 115, 123–126, 132, 134–135, 138, 162, 165–166, 168–169, 172–173, 175
Northwest Cove 6

O'Hearn, Patrick 130
Organ, Freeman 25
Osmond, Terry 156
Otter's Point 51
Outhouse, Glendon 154, 156

MV *Pacific Venture* 169
Pack, Almon J. 112
S/V *Paloma* 94
Parsons, Archibald 28, 30
Parsons, Arthur 67–69
Parsons, Harry 4
Parsons, Ronald 77
MV *Pat & David* 132
MV *Penny Luck II* 192

Penny, Cecil 199
MV *Pennyrowe* 178
MV *Percy F. Russell* 56–58, 60–61
Pero, Micheal 186
MV *Petite Forte* 191
Petit de Grau 125
Petites 5, 34–35, 56, 58, 63
Petro, Cecil 27
S/V *Pheobe A* 41
Philpott, Inez 35–36
Piercy, Garfield 118
Piercy, Richard 99–101
Pike, E. 50
Pink, Alvin 59
Pink, Berthina 88
Pink, Matthew 51
Pink, Roy 87–88
Pink, Walter 86, 88
Pink, Walter Sr. 59
Point Edward 59–60
Point Enragee 97
Point May 199
Poirier, Pierre 130
MV *Polly & Robbie* 165
Port au Port 13
Port Blandford 27
Port de Granville 28
Porter, Caroline 30
Porter, Harvey 69
Porter, John Robert 69
Portugal 63
Price, Alan 70
Price, Bert 70
MV *Primrose* 83
MV *Provo Wallis* 134
Purchase, Agnes 171–172
Purchase, Charles 60
Purchase, Christian Murray 175
Purchase, Duclie 172

CLARENCE VAUTIER JR. WAS BORN IN 1972 IN LA POILE, Newfoundland and Labrador. He moved away to attend high school, and after completion, he fished for a short time with his father, Clarence Sr., and his brother, Raymond. He later attended the Nautical Institute of Nova Scotia in Port Hawkesbury, Nova Scotia, where he obtained employment with Biorex Atlantic Inc., subsequently making numerous voyages on many fishing vessels on the east coast of Canada.

In 1994, he enrolled at the Institute of Fisheries and Marine Technology at Memorial University of Newfoundland in St. John's, where he studied navigation. He later went to work as a deck officer on the Great Lakes, first for P & H Shipping, then for Algoma Central Marine, where he remains today.

Clarence Vautier currently resides in St. John's with his wife, Marina, his son, Brandon, and his daughter, Hannah.